THE DECLINE OF THE BRITISH MOTOR INDUSTRY

The Decline of the British Motor Industry

The Effects of Government Policy, 1945-1979

Peter J.S. Dunnett

CROOM HELM LONDON

© 1980 Peter J.S. Dunnett
Croom Helm Ltd, 2-10 St John's Road, London SW11

British Library Cataloguing in Publication Data

Dunnett, Peter J S
    The decline of the British motor industry.
    1. Automobile industry and trade – Great Britain
    – History 2. Great Britain – Economic policy –
    1945-
    I. Title
    338.4'7'62920941   HD9710.G72

ISBN 0-7099-0012-0

Printed in Great Britain by
Biddles Ltd, Guildford, Surrey

CONTENTS

TABLES

FIGURES

TO BARBARA

PREFACE

This book analyses the role of the government in the relative decline of the United Kingdom's motor industry over the past thirty-five years. It attempts to cast light on how government policies played an important part in that decline. I hope that this case study of the UK motor industry will prove of some use to those, around the world, who are interested in policy and the consequences of policy for specific industries. I also hope the book will provide insights for those interested in both the UK motor industry and the post-war history of the UK government's economic and social policy.

In writing this book I owe a debt of thanks to too many people and institutions to mention them all. Dr Richard Schwindt of Simon Fraser University, Dr Colin Jones of the University of Victoria, Dr John Cubbin of Warwick University and Dr William Rodney of Royal Roads Military College were particularly helpful. Royal Roads Military College generously provided financial assistance. Mrs Helene Smith and Miss Velda Holland patiently typed the manuscripts. Last, but not least, my wife and family were ever tolerant.

1 INTRODUCTION

This book is about the government and the motor industry. It is about how the government, in attempting to achieve various economic, political and social objectives, used and abused, helped and hindered, and generally modified the United Kingdom motor industry, both through direct and indirect actions.

Such an undertaking immediately raises a number of basic questions: What were the government's overall objectives? How did the government attempt to achieve these objectives? What was the importance of the motor industry relative to these objectives? How, in turn, could government policies in pursuit of overall objectives affect the motor industry? These questions are briefly examined.

What Were the Government's Overall Economic Objectives?

Since 1945 the governments of the Western World have accepted a general responsibility for the performance of their economies, and in economic matters the goals which they have sought to achieve have been very similar. In Britain, the Radcliffe Report of 1959 stated the economic goals or overall objectives of the country as follows:[1]

1. Full employment
2. Economic growth
3. Price stability
4. Adequate balance of payment surplus ⎫
5. Adequate foreign reserves ⎭ — external balance
6. A desirable composition of output — allocative efficiency
7. A desirable distribution of income ⎫
8. Individual freedom of choice in economic matters ⎭ — equity

Economic policy, therefore, is a matter of attempting to achieve all these goals. Since this is impossible, given the current state of economics, such policy involves choosing by how much each goal should be sacrificed in order to gain that combination of outcomes which the government believes to be optimal. Whilst different British governments changed the emphasis given to each of these goals and set different priorities, the goals themselves have remained largely unaltered since 1945.

How Did the Government Attempt to Achieve its Objectives?

To achieve its objectives the government used economic policy instruments. Instruments might be of a general nature, such as a change in personal income tax affecting just about everybody, or of a more specific nature, such as a protective tariff on a particular sort of commodity, affecting only a small sector of the economy. Consequently it was possible for the implementation of policy to affect just about every segment of society, and in this book the emphasis is on the effects on the motor industry.

How Important Has the Motor Industry Been to the United Kingdom Economy?

Since World War II the motor industry has been a highly important leading sector in the British economy and, although in the private sector, has been very considerably influenced by government policy. A.G. Armstrong used input-output analysis to estimate the importance of the motor industry to the British economy.[2] Directly, he estimated, the motor industry accounted for (i) about five per cent of industrial production between 1954 and 1966, (ii) about nine per cent of growth in industrial production in the same period and (iii) about 15 per cent of the uneven character of growth in industrial production. Indirectly, the importance of the motor industry was about the same, its requirements from other industries amounting to 3.9 per cent of industrial production in 1954 and 5.5 per cent in 1966. Overall, this implies that the motor industry was responsible for about 11 per cent of industrial production between 1954 and 1966. Furthermore, because of faster than average growth in the motor industry, as compared to industrial production as a whole, 27 per cent of growth in industrial production between 1954 and 1966 was attributable to the motor industry's growth. In 1975 the Central Policy Review Staff published *The Future of the British Car Industry* which stated the belief that the motor industry was still responsible for about 11 per cent of industrial output.[3] Slower than average growth in the UK motor industry implied a smaller contribution to the overall growth in industrial production between 1966 and 1979 than in earlier years (see Table 1.1).

Table 1.1: United Kingdom Motor Industry Investment as a Percentage of Investment in all UK Manufacturing Industries, 1963-72

Year	Percentage
1963	10
1964	8
1965	8
1966	8
1967	8
1968	7
1969	7
1970	8
1971	6
1972	5

Source: National Economic Development Office, *Industrial Review to 1977, Motors*, p. 32.

How Could the Motor Industry Contribute to the Government's Overall Economic Objectives?

The motor industry's potential ability to contribute to the achievement of the government's overall economic objectives is quite straightforward. A vital and efficient motor industry is a provider of jobs and creator of incomes so contributing to full employment.

Table 1.2: Total Direct Employment in the Motor Industry, Selected Years

Year	Number (thousands)
1948	284
1954	312
1960	435
1973	508

Sources: Central Statistical Office, *Annual Abstract of Statistics*; Parliament (Commons), *Fourteenth Report of the Expenditure Committee, 1974-75: The Motor Vehicle Industry* (HMSO, London, 1975), p. 48.

It also produces a product with a high income elasticity of demand, so that as per capita incomes increase, car demand increases more than proportionately and becomes yet more important to final demand in the economy: a prosperous motor industry is likely, therefore, to be a substantial contributor to economic growth. As an industry where opportunities for large productivity increases have traditionally been found, it is potentially capable of paying higher wages without experiencing increasing costs, so contributing to price stability and rising living standards. As an export industry it can help the balance of payments and the accumulation of foreign reserves. Operating at full capacity and structured to exploit available economies of scale, the industry can contribute to productive and allocative efficiency to produce a desirable composition of output. Finally, as a high wage industry it may contribute to a desirable distribution of income and, if it enjoys workable competition, provide choice to the consumer. The ability of the motor industry to make these contributions to the achievement of the goals set out by the Radcliffe Committee depends upon the structure, conduct and performance of the industry. By introducing policies which alter these, a government can move towards or away from any of its particular overall economic objectives.

How Could Government Policies in Pursuit of Overall Objectives Affect the Motor Industry, Either Directly or Indirectly?

Government policy affected the motor industry in three different ways. First, policies were aimed directly and specifically at the motor industry in order to achieve a particular goal. For example, in 1960 the government refused industrial development certificates to the motor industry in order to force the industry to relocate in areas of high unemployment. Here was a policy specifically applied to the motor industry, causing a fundamental geographical relocation, in order to provide greater equity in the distribution of income. Secondly, policies were aimed at a broader sector of the economy but still had a direct influence on the motor industry. For example, the government frequently used hire purchase restrictions on all consumer durables including cars as a means of controlling aggregate demand. At times this caused excess capacity to develop in the motor industry raising unit costs and affecting industry performance. Thirdly, policies were made which only indirectly affected the motor industry. For example, after the war, following the Beveridge Report, the British government committed itself to high priority for the social services. As a result, expenditures on transport, in general, were neglected. One facet of this neglect was very low expenditures on the roads. Consequently, British cars were designed for an antiquated road system and were unsuitable for the more modern highways found in many export markets. Thus, as a result of the government stressing social services and the overall equity goal, the motor industry made a smaller contribution to the balance of payments and economic growth than might otherwise have occurred.

This book undertakes to examine the adequacy of government policies as they affected the motor industry. Alternatively, its aim can be put in the following form. Between 1945 and 1979 the British motor industry suffered a dramatic relative decline in efficiency, competitiveness and world importance. Government policy strongly influenced structure, conduct and performance in the motor industry. These facts raise two questions. First, was government policy between 1945 and 1979 to any extent a cause of this decline, as opposed to having a neutral or restraining influence on the decline? If the answer to the first question is in the affirmative it still raises a second question. Was this relative decline in the one industry a worthwhile sacrifice in that it made it possible for the government to attain more closely its overall economic objectives?

This book seeks to provide a full long-run economic analysis of how post-war government policy permeated through to affect almost all aspects of the conditions in which the UK motor industry operated. To date, commentators have tended to concentrate either on labour relations and management in the motor industry or on the nature of the product. For the past decade the media has been rife with reports about impossible trade union demands, incompetent management, the generally poor quality of British cars and the weak overall performance of the UK motor industry. In this book it is argued that often labour and management problems, which frequently received the attention in criticism of the UK motor industry, were themselves not causes but symptoms, and that often the cause of their problems was to be found in government economic policies. Nevertheless, the importance of the effect of government policy on the UK motor industry has not gone completely unnoticed. In 1956 Roy Jenkins, later British Home Secretary and President of the European Economic Community, said,

> In every conceivable way the future of the motor industry is bound up not only in its ability to solve its own problems but with the framework within which the government are to allow it to apply to these problems . . . the industry is operating within a constantly changing framework and will continue to do so in the future, and the authority that determines that framework is the government.[4]

And a decade later *The Times* with singular foresight commented,

> Too many factors depend on [the motor industry] . . . for any government to ignore its general health or neglect to provide the conditions in which it can thrive.[5]

At the outset it should be made clear that the purpose of this book is not simply to attack government intervention with the benefit of hindsight. It is hoped the book provides a learning exercise. Certainly, as will be seen, the government made mistakes, and in some circumstances policy is found to be weak. The aim of the book, however, is to analyse where policy was successful and where it was lacking in the particular context of the motor industry in order to provide answers to the following questions. Where policy failed, did it fail because the policy objectives were wrong? Or because the execution of the policy was inept? Or because although the objective was reasonable and the execution of policy adequate, unforeseen circumstances or side effects arose to offset favourable policy outcomes? Whilst it can be quite entertaining to indulge in attacks on government policy, government policy failures tend to be expensive. If, as a result of studies such as this, similar failures in the future can be avoided and similar successes replicated then such exercises have some productive use.

Notes

1. M. Lipton, *The British Economy, 1945-68* (Staples Press, London, 1968), p. 27.
2. A.C. Armstrong, 'The Motor Industry and the British Economy', *District Bank Review*, 164 (Sept. 1967), pp. 19-40.
3. Central Policy Review Staff, *The Future of the British Car Industry* (HMSO, London, 1975), p. 9.
4. R. Jenkins, House of Commons Debates (hereafter HCD), 22 Feb. 1957, col. 800.
5. *The Times*, 25 May 1967.

2 THE NATURE OF THE POST-WAR MOTOR INDUSTRY

Before commencing the analysis of the effects of government policy on the UK motor industry some background is necessary. Firstly, the important features of the British motor industry since 1945 are discussed. Then the method of analysis used in subsequent chapters is briefly outlined. Fuller descriptions of both can be found elsewhere.[1] The purpose here is to provide the reader unfamiliar with the UK motor industry and the field of industrial organisation sufficient general knowledge to follow the fairly straightforward arguments of the main chapters. Readers familiar with both may wish to read just the summary at the end of this chapter.

The Motor Industry Since 1945

Basic Conditions

The basic market conditions of any industry refer to the essential determinants and characteristics of market supply and demand.

Supply. Well before World War II the main features determining supply by the UK motor industry had been established. The nature of the product and the basic technology covering product design and methods of production had been clearly defined and no radical technical innovations were to be expected in the following years. The car, powered by the internal combustion engine, had proven itself to be a desirable means of private transport with considerable product durability dependent upon usage and, to some extent, fashion-induced obsolescence. During the pre-war years a failure to earn profits had weeded out a large number of would-be producers; nevertheless, in 1945, many still survived. Trade unions had been accepted into some factories before wartime legislation had forced the remainder to recognise unions. Unionisation had occurred along the traditional craft lines; consequently in every factory in 1945 the workforce was represented by a number of unions. In terms of the final value of the product the value of imported materials used was low.

Demand. The British motor industry received demand from two distinct markets, the home market and the overseas market.

In 1945, in the home market, the car was still largely a middle and upper income group luxury. At the time it was questioned whether Britain would ever achieve the levels of car ownership of the United States, given Britain's density of population and comprehensive rail and bus network. On the other hand, many of the middle and upper income classes who could afford a car owned one. Since it was unlikely that those income groups had a monopoly on tastes for private transportation, it was reasonable to believe, in 1945, that future economic growth would generate increasing car demand among middle and lower income groups. Nevertheless, the existence of a large number of substitutes for new cars — second-hand cars, motorcycles, and public transport — meant that people could easily postpone new car purchases. Added to a seasonal demand for cars, these factors meant that car demand was likely to be as unstable in the home market in the following years as it had been before the war. The home market was characterised by considerable brand loyalty among customers. Before World War II engine taxation policies and protective duties had given the UK manufacturers a virtual monopoly of the home market, but had encouraged the production of designs largely illsuited to overseas markets. Consequently the overseas market had been relatively neglected and between the wars less than ten per cent of production had been exported. Despite the existence of imperial preference, which imposed lower tariffs on British cars in the Commonwealth, American cars had still outsold British cars there. In non-Commonwealth markets before the war there had been stiff competition from the French, Germans and Italians. After World War II the fact that the home market was protected and captive, whilst most overseas markets were more competitive, enabled the UK manufacturers to indulge in price discrimination between the home and overseas markets.

Structure

The structure of an industry describes such things as the number of sellers, the ease with which new firms can enter the industry, the nature of costs for firms, the degree of vertical integration and the extent of product differentiation.

A car is made up of about twenty thousand parts. To enable a meaningful discussion of the structure of the British motor industry since 1945 it is first necessary to define the industry for our purposes. Since the vast majority of the twenty thousand parts are purchased from components suppliers by the motor industry a more appropriate name for the so-called motor manufacturers might be designers and assemblers. A problem for this analysis is that whereas some producers of parts and components produce only for the motor industry, a great many of the others provide, or could provide, parts to the rest of the engineering industry. Bearings, nuts and bolts, electrical parts, plastic parts, trim, materials, rubber parts and so on are by no means used exclusively in the motor industry. And, whilst some of the suppliers of those items are tied in to the industry, many others are not and could survive without any motor business. Accordingly, in order to define the limits of the structure of the industry for this analysis a brief discussion of vertical integration in the industry is required.

Vertical Integration. Around the world different motor companies in different countries have demonstrated widely different degrees of vertical integration. In the UK, the existence of a large number of machine shops in the Midlands at the turn of the century meant an embryo components industry already existed. Over the years as the motor industry grew so did the components industry so that, in comparison to American and European producers, the UK motor industry has been generally characterised by a lack of vertical integration, and has brought in many of its supplies rather than manufacture them itself.[2]

To the extent that vertical integration had occurred by the end of World War II, firm size was less important than other factors, notably expediency. For example, the small Armstrong Siddely company, a subsidiary of the aeroplane manufacturer Hawker Siddely, used to produce a high proportion of its own components. And, whilst Vauxhall produced its own bodies and electrical parts in the forties, Ford brought in these parts but, unlike Vauxhall, had its own foundry. The lack of vertical integration in the industry meant that the largest supply companies, such as Pressed Steel (bodies), Joseph Lucas (electrics) and Dunlop (wheels, tyres and rubber products), were comparable to the large manufacturers in terms of capital and labour employed.

Table 2.1: Specimen Percentages of Material Cost of Cars Accounted for by Bought-out Components, 1973

GM (US)	46
Ford (US)	61
Toyota	59
BLMC	65
Ford (UK)	70
Chrysler (UK)	71
Vauxhall	85

Source: Parliament (Commons), *Fourteenth Report of the Expenditure Committee, 1974-75: The Motor Vehicle Industry* (HMSO, London, 1975), p. 19.

The lack of vertical integration provided three advantages to the motor manufacturers. Firstly, it freed capital, which would have been used to produce parts, for other purposes. Secondly, often as virtual monopsonists, the motor manufacturers were able to put pressure on a supplier to get parts at prices equal to, or less than, the costs it would have incurred to produce the parts themselves. Predatory tactics were not unknown. Ford, for example, would award profitable contracts to small components suppliers who would be encouraged to abandon other customers. Once dependent upon Ford, Ford would then squeeze profit margins. Thirdly, a lack of integration gave the manufacturers greater flexibility. When trade boomed it was possible to bring in other suppliers on a temporary basis who could be dropped when trade slowed.

For the purposes of this study the motor industry refers to the motor manufacturers, the final assemblers and sellers of cars. Whilst much of the analysis is applicable to the components industry, and whilst performance of the components industry was heavily dependent upon that of the car industry, it is not directly examined.

Number of Firms and Models. In 1945 in the UK there were still dozens of specialist car manufacturers, such as A-C, Allard, Alvis, Armstrong Siddely and Aston Martin. However, six manufacturers controlled nearly ninety per cent of UK production. These were the so-called 'big six' of Austin, Morris (Nuffield), Rootes, Standard, Ford and Vauxhall (GM). Also with a significant share of the market were Rover, Jaguar, Jowett and Singer. Production shares for selected years are shown in Table 2.2.

Table 2.2: Shares of UK Car Production by UK Manufacturers, Selected Years (Percentage)

Manufacturer				1947	1954	1960	1974	1978
Morris	BMC	BMH	BL	20.9	38.0	36.5	48.2	50.0
Austin				19.2	–	–	–	–
Jaguar				1.6	1.5	1.7	–	–
Standard		Leyland		13.2	11.0	8.0	–	–
Rover				2.7	1.7	1.6	–	–
Rootes-Chrysler		Chrysler		10.9	11.0	10.6	10.9	16.1
Singer				2.1	–	–	–	–
Vauxhall				11.2	9.0	10.7	8.9	6.9
Ford				15.4	27.0	30.0	25.0	26.5

Sources: Parliament (Commons), *Fourteenth Report of the Expenditure Committee, 1974-75: The Motor Vehicle Industry* (HMSO, London, 1975), p. 378; Parliament (Commons), *Eighth Report of the Expenditure Committee, 1975-76: Public Expenditure on Chrysler (UK)* (HMSO, London, 1976), p. 30; SMMT data.

Following World War II the UK motor industry contained a large number of producers compared to the United States or the European countries. To a large extent the number of surviving producers, and the proliferation of models which had occurred before the war, can be traced to the RAC horsepower taxation system and the nature of competition. These had fragmented the market and so encouraged the larger manufacturers to make many models, thereby forsaking economies of scale and the potential ability to lower unit costs. As a result, smaller specialist producers had a greater opportunity to compete.

Economies of Scale. Manufacturers are naturally reluctant to provide data about their costs so that an empirical study of the relationship between costs and output can be made. Nevertheless, several experts since 1939 have made estimates about the nature of the long-run cost curve (the way unit costs rise or fall as production volume increases) for motor vehicle production. These studies have emphasised production economies of scale, although some evidence on firm economies (economies in such non-production areas as marketing and finance) has also been gathered. Economies of scale play a significant role in the analysis of this book.

First, production economies are examined. Table 2.3 summarises the results of studies to measure production economies of scale. In all studies researchers examined the optimum outputs of various stages of motor vehicle production; engine manufacture, body pressings and assembly. The minimum efficient scale of output per year (MES) for car production depends upon economies of scale being exploited at all stages of production. Although there is considerable variation in the results of these studies shown in Table 2.3 much of this variation can be explained.

The low estimates of the British Manufacturers Advisory Council (BMAC) in 1950, of Paul Hoffman, President of the Studebaker Motor Company before the Temporary National Economic Committee (TNEC) in 1939, and of George Romney, President of American Motors, quoted by Edwards in 1965, were all made by company spokesmen representing organisations which were too small to exploit all available economies of scale, by their own recognition. Consequently, all these estimates were no more than informed guesses, possibly even optimistic wishful thinking: it must have been very tempting for all of them to genuinely believe that if only they could increase their production a little their competitive position would improve greatly. Boyle's low estimate in 1976 comes from an argument in which he proposes breaking up the large American

Table 2.3: Production Economies of Scale in the Motor Industry

MES	Year	Country	Technical Stage Determining MES	Source	Cost Penalty (at 50% MES)
100,000	1939	USA	Pressings	TNEC[a]	
100,000	1950	UK	Pressings	BMAC[b]	
250,000	1950	UK	Pressings	APE[c]	
150,000	1954	UK	Pressings	*The Economist*[d]	
1,000,000	1954	UK	Pressings	Maxcy & Silbertson[e]	
1,200,000	1955	UK	Pressings	Wansbrough[f]	20%
600,000	1956	USA	Pressings & Machinings	Bain[g]	
1,500,000	1962	UK	Pressings	Menje[h]	
400,000	1965	USA	Pressings	Edwards[i]	
800,000	1969	USA	Pressings	White[j]	5%
1,000,000	1969	UK	Pressings	Pratten & Deane[k]	13%
2,000,000	1971	UK	Pressings	Rhys[l]	
4,000,000	1972	USA	Pressings	McGee[m]	
1,750,000	1975	UK	Pressings	CPRS[n]	
250,000	1976	USA	Assembly	Boyle[o]	
2,000,000	1975	UK	Foundry	Beckett[p]	

Sources:
(a) United States Senate. Temporary National Economic Committee. Part 21 (6 Dec. 1939), p. 11199.
(b) British Manufacturers Advisory Council, quoted in *The Economist*, 1 Dec. 1951, p. 1348.
(c) American Production Engineers.
(d) *The Economist*, 23 Oct. 1954, pp. 7-11.
(e) G. Maxcy and A. Silbertson, *The Motor Industry* (Allen and Unwin, London, 1958), p. 93.
(f) G. Wansbrough, 'Automobiles: The Mass Market', *Lloyds Bank Review*, Oct. 1955, p. 32.
(g) J. Bain, *Barriers to New Competition* (Harvard University Press, Cambridge, Mass., 1956), p. 78.
(h) J.A. Menje, 'Style Change Costs as A Market Weapon', *Quarterly Journal of Economics*, 76, Nov. 1962, pp. 632-47.
(i) C.E. Edwards, *Dynamics of the United States Automobile Industry* (University of South Carolina Press, Columbia, 1965), p. 153.
(j) L.J. White, *The Automobile Industry Since 1945* (Harvard University Press, Cambridge, Mass., 1971), p. 53.
(k) C.F. Pratten, *Economies of Scale in Manufacturing Industry* (Cambridge University Press, Cambridge, 1971), p. 243.
(l) D.G. Rhys, *The Motor Industry: An Economic Survey* (Butterworths, London, 1972), p. 291.
(m) *Fortune*, 7 May 1979, p. 128.
(n) Central Policy Review Staff, *The Future of the British Car Industry* (HMSO, London, 1975), p. 14.

(o) S.E. Boyle, 'A Blueprint for Competition: Restructuring the Motor Vehicle Industry', *Journal of Economic Issues*, IX (June 1975), p. 260.

(p) Parliament (Commons), *Fourteenth Report of the Expenditure Committee, 1974-75: The Motor Vehicle Industry* (HMSO, London, 1975), p. 37.

automobile companies in order to generate competition. Boyle acknowledges technical economies of scale in forgings and pressings beyond his figures, but argues that in the United States separate companies could supply forgings and pressings. Comments by researchers provide some explanation for the variation in the estimates of economies of scale in pressings. The life expectancy of a die for pressing depends upon the nature of the pressing involved. The more the metal sheet has to be stretched, the shorter the lifetime of the die. By the seventies a die could be expected to last for up to seven million presses. On the assumption of a four-year model life, economies of scale in excess of one million are implied, depending upon designs. By extending model lifespans and using common pressings between models some reduction in economies of scale in this area can be made.

This brief assessment of studies of the long-run cost curve for car output concludes that in the late forties product economies of scale exceeded 150,000 units per year. In the fifties, automatic transfer machines and unitary body construction had raised this figure considerably, probably to above 500,000 units. In the sixties this figure increased towards a million, and in the seventies exceeded one million. In Table 2.4 a comparison is made between these estimates of the minimum efficient scale of production and the output of Britain's largest manufacturer, for selected years. In no year did any British company achieve sufficient production to exploit all potential economies of scale in production.

Table 2.4: Relationship Between Minimum Efficient Scale of Production (MES) and Largest British Motor Firm's Size, Selected Years

Year	Largest Firm's Production Share*	Total Production	Estimate of Largest Firm's Production**	MES	MES/Estimate
1947	21%	287,000	60,000	150,000	.4
1954	38%	769,000	292,000	600,000	.5
1960	36%	1,352,000	486,000	750,000	.6
1967	45%	1,552,000	700,000	1,000,000	.7
1974	48%	1,543,000	740,000	1,250,000	.6
1977	49%	1,315,000	651,000	2,000,000	.3

* For Years: 1947, Nuffield; 1954, BMC; 1960, BMC; 1967, BMH; 1974, BL; 1978, BL
**Actual production figures not available
Sources: SMMT, *The Motor Industry of Great Britain*, various years; Table 2.2.

Secondly, firm economies of scale are examined. There is some evidence suggesting firm economies at yet higher levels of production. These are presented in Table 2.5. Adequate sales network coverage, advertising, finance, risk minimisation, fashion, and research and development all offer the opportunity for lowering unit costs once all product economies have been exhausted. During the seventies Volvo, Saab and Fiat introduced methods of production which abandoned the assembly line and instead had cars assembled by small groups in an attempt to eliminate monotony for the workers and quality control problems for the manufacturers. These production method changes might suggest a car company can become too big and experience diseconomies of scale. However, reports on these experiments concluded that none of them lowered costs for the firms, and a more successful way to eliminate the monotonous jobs, so familiar in the motor industry, would appear to be through more automation, for example, the automatic welding machines General Motors introduced at its Lordstown, Ohio, plant.

Table 2.5: Firm Economies of Scale in the UK Motor Industry

Year	Area	Approx. Scale (annual volumes)	Source
1956	Advertising[i]	500,000	Bain[a]
1957	Advertising[ii]	Significant	Weiss[b]
1961	Sales[iii]	1,800,000	Pashigan[c]
1970	Risks[iv]	800,000	White[d]
1971	Fashion[v]	Significant	Scherer[e]
1976	Finance[vi]	Significant	Cubbin[f]
1976	Research & Develop.[vii]	Significant	*Daily Telegraph*[g]
1976	Sales[viii]	5,000,000	Dunnett
1979	Research & Develop.[ix]	5,000,000	*Fortune*[h]

Notes:
(i)   Bain found significant economies of scale in advertising but doubted whether they exceeded United States production economies of 600,000 units annually.
(ii) Weiss calculated that Ford and GM spent $27 per car sold between 1954 and 1957; Chrysler $48; American Motors $58; Studebaker $64.
(iii) Pashigan estimated that an adequate sale and service network for the United States required annual sales volumes up to 1,800,000 units annually.
(iv) White noted that to remove undue risk a firm needed to offer at least two models at the same time. If production economies were virtually exhausted at 400,000 units annually, a firm must produce 800,000 units annually to safeguard itself against market failure such as the Edsel or Austin 1800.
(v)   Scherer notes that cars are fashion items. The faster dies are written off the greater the fashion advantage to the producer. In the US GM has shorter model runs than the other manufacturers.
(vi) Cubbin found that large UK companies had easier access to capital markets

at lower prices.

(vii) In 1976 newspapers reported that Ford spent $500m to develop the Ford Fiesta. With a four-year model run, annual volumes of the Fiesta will have to exceed one million if research and development expenses per car are to be below $100. At half that volume, unit costs per car will rise by about four per cent solely because of increased research costs per car.

(viii) An approximate estimate made by applying Pashigan's figures to the world car park.

(ix) *Fortune* magazine stated that economies of scale exceeded GM's total output for 1979.

Sources:

(a) J. Bain, *Barriers to New Competition* (Harvard University Press, Cambridge, Mass., 1956), p. 238.

(b) L. Weiss, *Economics and American Industry* (Wiley, New York, 1961), p. 342.

(c) B.P. Pashigan, *The Distribution of Automobiles: An Economic Analysis of the Franchise System* (Prentice-Hall, Englewood Cliffs, 1961), p. 126.

(d) L.J. White, *The Automobile Industry Since 1945* (Harvard University Press, Cambridge, Mass., 1971).

(e) F.M. Scherer, *Industrial Market Structure and Economic Performance* (Rand McNally, Chicago, 1973), p. 97.

(f) J. Cubbin, 'Mergers Project Case Study', Warwick University paper, Warwick, 1976, p. 27.

(g) *Daily Telegraph*, 30 July 1976.

(h) *Fortune*, 7 May 1979, p. 132.

In the light of this discussion and the results shown in Tables 2.3 and 2.5, it is deduced that the long-run average cost curve for UK producers, over the relevant range between 1945 and 1979, sloped downwards. In other words, and most importantly, it meant that, other things being equal, the more cars a manufacturer produced the cheaper it became on a per unit basis. The larger a manufacturer, the lower would be his costs relative to smaller rivals and the stronger his competitive position. The relationship between unit costs and output is shown in Figure 2.1.

Barriers to Entry. In any market a seller has to take cognisance of the possible effects of potential as well as existing rivals. In the post-war years considerable barriers to entry into the British motor industry existed which made it difficult for new firms to enter the market. Whilst a few specialist companies did enter the industry, for example Bristol in 1948 and Delorean in 1978, no specialist company grew to become a mass producer between 1945 and 1979. First, economies of scale provided very significant barriers to entry. A new entrant had to begin on a massive scale or else suffer considerable cost handicaps compared to larger established firms. Secondly, the mass producers had created barriers to entry through product differentiation. Over the years,

Figure 2.1: The Nature of Long-run Costs in Car Production

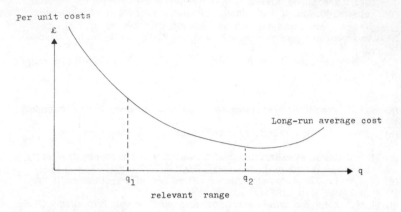

advertising and consumers' experiences with the different products had created considerable amounts of brand loyalty. In addition, with an expensive consumer durable such as a car most consumers are reluctant to experiment with an unknown quantity. Consequently, potential entrants were exposed to the risk that even a superior product might not be accepted by the public. Thirdly, established manufacturers enjoyed some absolute cost advantages in retailing. Most of the best retail locations and retailers were tied to an individual manufacturer. New entrants would have had to use inferior locations or bid away current retailers from established manufacturers. With reference to the purchase of components there is no evidence that established manufacturers enjoyed any cost advantages. Finally, as regards competition from foreign entrants the hefty McKenna duties created a formidable barrier to entry to the British market on a large scale up until at least the mid-1960s.

Conduct

Firm conduct or behaviour refers to such matters as pricing behaviour, the use of advertising, product strategies and the extent and role of research and innovation in the competitive process. The significant characteristics of firm conduct in the motor industry in 1945 are briefly summarised: they affected pricing, the nature of competition and co-operation between sellers.

As regards pricing behaviour the existence of two distinct markets enabled price discrimination. The captive home market had long been regarded as the major market and the main source of profits. In normal conditions prices were set such that at standard planning volumes home market prices covered full costs.[3] The more competitive and uncertain overseas market was regarded in a secondary light as a market which might absorb excess capacity, when necessary, and in which prices were set at levels which made some contribution to fixed costs. In other words, British firms followed a fairly standard practice of selling cars in overseas markets at below the full cost charged in the home market. In the home market, competition between firms took on non-price forms. Price cuts and price wars had been virtually unknown before World War II and were rarely encountered in the post-war era. Rather, manufacturers competed through such means as model designs, quality, reliability, service networks, advertising and the extent of standardised equipment. In order to cover the whole market UK manufacturers tended to produce a complete model range despite the negative effects of this on costs. Restrictive Trade Practices legislation and Resale Price Maintenance served to restrain competition between retailers since most retailers for the 'big six' were tied to a single manufacturer and, until 1956, were compelled by law to sell at list prices. The need for wartime co-operation and association through the Society of Motor Manufacturers and Traders meant that strong formal and informal networks of communication existed between the motor manufacturers. After the war the government encouraged the extension of inter-firm co-operation through public and private bodies, a development which is discussed in the following chapters in more detail.

Performance

In Chapter 1 the potential of the UK motor industry to contribute to the country's overall economic goals was outlined. In 1945 this potential was not being fully exploited. The nature of the long-run average cost curve for individual firms meant that the larger UK firms, if they exploited potential economies of scale, were in a strong position not only to make the more efficient use of scarce resources, but also to generate above industry average profits. To the extent that no firm exploited all available economies of scale the motor industry misallocated resources. In 1945 the largest companies were also, if efficient, in the strongest position to generate investment funds for growth and expansion. Britain does not have investment banks such as exist in France, Germany and Japan. Investment funds have to come from ploughed back profits and outside lenders. Typically, outside lenders lend to profitable companies.

Hence, in Britain, profits were a necessary prerequisite to growth and expansion. As regards employment, it was suggested in Chapter 1 that in the post-war era the motor industry was a powerful generator of employment. However, the discussion of demand above shows that demand was affected by seasonal and cyclical factors so making the industry an unreliable labour market. Until 1945 the motor industry had not made a significant contribution to the balance of payments.

Method of Analysis

In this book a method of analysis frequently used to explain how industrial organisations operate is followed. It is presented diagramatically in Figure 2.2. How satisfactorily any industry performs is seen as depending upon its basic conditions of supply and demand, the industry's structure, and the industry's conduct or behaviour.

Figure 2.2: An Industrial Organisation Analytical Model

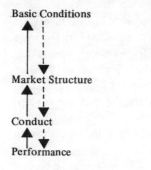

Basic Conditions

Supply: raw materials; technology; product durability; business attitudes; firm attitudes.
Demand: price elasticity; rate of growth; substitutes; marketing type; purchase method; cyclical and seasonal fluctuations.

Market Structure

Number of buyers and sellers; product differentiation; barriers to entry; cost structure; vertical integration; conglomerates.

Conduct

Pricing behaviour; product strategy; research and innovation; advertising; legal tactics.

Performance

Production and allocative efficiency; progress; full employment; equity; external balance.

Source: F.M. Scherer, *Industrial Market Structure and Economic Performance* (Rand McNally, Chicago, 1976), p. 4.

Using this technique any given government policy examined in this book will usually be seen to affect basic conditions and thence have repercussions upon industry structure, conduct and finally performance. However, it is quite possible that a government policy will have its initial impact on structure or on conduct. Also this analytical approach does not exclude the possibility of performance having feedback effects on basic conditions, structure and conduct, and on government policy itself. One example of a feedback effect as a result of industry performance occurred in 1947. An export drive, which affected supply, was instigated by the government to help the balance of payments. The nature of the export drive meant an increased export of cars was accompanied by inadequate spare parts and service back-up. Consequently, when some overseas consumers could not obtain spare parts for their cars they swore never to buy British again, and so overseas demand in later years was decreased. Similarly, the initial overall success of this export drive encouraged the government to apply further pressure to the industry to export yet more. However, as will be shown in the subsequent chapters, the main effects of government policy on the motor industry, since 1945, were transmitted from changes in basic conditions through structure and conduct to performance.

Whilst government policy will be seen to have had considerable effects on the development of the UK motor industry, the ability of the industry to affect government policy was limited. Although not totally impotent, other political considerations limited the influence of the motor industry lobby. The efforts of the motor industry to affect government policy are discussed as they arise but in most cases will be found to have had limited success.

Summary

The method of analysis to be used in this book is the chronological evaluation of the effects of government policy on the basic conditions, structure, conduct and performance of the motor industry. In the late forties, when the analysis begins, the basic conditions of supply and demand in the motor industry were as follows. Two distinct markets made price discrimination possible. In the future, demand was likely to be unstable but, if economic growth occurred, to show an upward trend in the home market. On the supply side, profit-motivated firms, recently unionised, used an accepted technology to produce a durable commodity with low import content. Industry structure was dominated by six major mass manufacturers of cars, none of which was large enough to exploit all economies of scale, and all of which were heavily reliant on the components industry for minor and major parts. Barriers to entry for potential entrants were high. Industry conduct was characterised by considerable co-operation and collusion, the ability to discriminate in price between the protected home market and overseas markets, and non-price competition in the home market. In terms of overall economic goals, the motor industry, as structured in 1945, did not exploit its full potential in terms of allocative efficiency, stable employment and its contribution to the balance of payments.

Notes

1. D.G. Rhys, *The Motor Industry: An Economic Survey* (Butterworths, London, 1972); F.M. Scherer, *Industrial Market Structure and Economic Performance* (Rand McNally, Chicago, 1970).

2. K. Richardson, *The British Motor Industry 1896-1939: A Social and Economic History* (Macmillan, London, 1977), pp. 90-1.

3. Standard planning volumes refer to a production schedule based on regular full-time working but excluding working weekends, public holidays and overtime.

3 POST-WAR DEVELOPMENTS: AN APPARENT SUCCESS, 1945-52

When World War II ended, the huge task of reconverting the wartime economy to peacetime purposes began. This required considerable government involvement in most sectors of the economy for many years, an involvement in no way diminished by the 1945 Labour government's election pledges of more economic planning and intervention. This process of transition to a peacetime economy was still in progress when the Korean War broke out in 1950 and the government felt compelled to undertake a policy of rearmament once again.

In this chapter we examine how government policies dealing with post-war reconversion and the Korean crisis affected the motor industry. Policies concerned with exports, rearmament requirements, taxation, rationing and distribution, transportation, monopolies and labour relations are analysed.

Export Policy

Once Allied victory seemed likely the government began to consider post-war economic policy. One area of key concern was Britain's likely international financial position after the war. Clearly, as a result of the sacrifices made to finance the war effort, Britain's income from abroad would be considerably diminished as compared to pre-war levels, and unless successful remedial action was taken there would be balance of payments difficulties and pressures on sterling in the following years. Accordingly the government created machinery to mount an export drive for the immediate post-war era.

Initially, the major emphasis of the government's plan for a post-war export drive was the traditional export industries such as textiles. The motor industry was not included. The reason for this was simple. Before World War II the motor industry had focused its attention on the home market and had made only a small contribution to exports. However, once the war ended it became apparent that the motor industry would be able to make a most valuable contribution to the post-war export drive. Around the world many markets had been starved of consumer durables, including cars, for five years. There was a sellers market. Car manufacturers in the United States, by far the world's largest producer of cars at that time, could not even meet home demand so that, with the European car producers still in disarray because of war damage, it was clear a considerable opportunity for the UK manufacturers existed overseas. Hastily the government included the motor industry in its export drive and created an export policy for the motor industry. The President of the Board of Trade announced the new policy at the Society of Motor Manufacturers and Traders (SMMT) 1946 dinner. Astounded, industry representatives heard they would be required to export fifty per cent of production. To implement the new policy and supervise the industry the government set up a manufacturer-dominated National Advisory Council under the auspices of the Minister of Supply. But the government's real control over the motor industry stemmed from its monopoly over scarce resource supplies, particularly steel. The government merely had to threaten to cut these off, if manufacturers did not satisfactorily attempt to meet export quotas, to gain compliance.

In the following years the government called for further increases in car exports as it implemented its export drive. The motor industry proved to be one of the country's most capable foreign currency earners.

A brief history of the export quota system runs as follows. Initial success in meeting the export targets for 1946 persuaded the government to raise them for 1947. Meeting the higher targets proved difficult. Already extremely harsh weather early in 1947 had created shortages of fuel and steel hampering production and exports when, in July, sterling was made freely convertible. This had disastrous effects on British car exports. Foreign buyers in the sterling area could now obtain previously scarce dollars to purchase generally preferred American cars. Though convertibility was suspended in August the pressure on sterling continued. In response, the government introduced further efforts to stimulate exports. Initially, car export quotas were raised to seventy-five per cent of production, but later the government reserved all output for export except that required to meet 'essential' home demand. Nevertheless, the President of the Board of Trade, Mr Harold Wilson, had to revise downwards projected exports as actual exports lagged well below the quotas. By 1948 the pound had become overvalued and, at the same time, some international competition from the Americans and also the French had developed. Early in 1949, when less than two-thirds of car production was being exported, the government modified the quotas so that,

> In order to give the manufacturers greater flexibility, they will no longer be required to keep rigidly within quarterly allocations for the home market so long as their exports over a reasonable period attain the required level.[1]

Marshall Aid helped to stimulate the world economy that year with some short-term beneficial effects on export demand for British cars, but exports were still well below original targets. Devaluation in September 1949 completely altered the situation and by mid-1950 exports accounted for over four-fifths of production and the export drive was as strong as at any time in the post-war era. Unfortunately before the opportunities of devaluation could be fully exploited the government's export policy was sharply modified. The Korean crisis had developed in June 1950 and as part of its North Atlantic Treaty Organisation (NATO) commitment the government introduced a rearmament policy which had priority over the export drive and the attempt to achieve a satisfactory balance of payments.

Basically, therefore, the government's post-war export policy for the motor industry was one of establishing export quotas, then relaxing these whenever difficulties in meeting the quotas arose. On the surface such a policy might not seem to be particularly consequential. Nevertheless, it was. The policy had very considerable effects on the industry's structure, conduct and performance, which had repercussions long after the export policy itself was abandoned. These are now examined.

Effects on Basic Conditions

Before World War II the UK motor industry had been the largest in Europe. It had also come out of the war relatively unscathed when compared to the French, German and Italian industries. When the government's export policy was introduced, therefore, the UK industry was clearly foremost in Europe. By early 1946 all the large UK companies had completed the major part of reconversion from war production and the ability to produce was limited less by capacity than by uncertain supplies of coal and steel from the government. Indeed, throughout the years of the export drive the short supplies of essential raw materials, under government control, were the main constraints on output.

Following the war a worldwide shortage of dollars made it impossible for many overseas buyers to acquire American cars. Consequently, given the state of the European industry, the British motor industry held a virtual monopoly over the many would-be buyers who held sterling. Nevertheless, in 1946 it was impossible to estimate the extent of overseas demand. Two very important factors were unknown: first, the effect of the war on people's income, wealth and consumption patterns; second, the condition of the world stock of cars. Still, the British government was persuaded to believe that there was 'an almost illimitable demand for these vehicles'.[2] Europe, the Far East, India, Russia and the

Commonwealth were regarded as potential markets and one estimate even went so far as to suggest the Russians would require twenty million vehicles over the following five years.[3] The motor industry was less optimistic and more concerned about for how long demand would continue for British cars which were mostly pre-war models and designed for Britain's undemanding road system. Although in the post-war years British cars sold well where American cars were unavailable, and to a limited extent where the existing demand was for small cars, a price-quality comparison showed the Americans' clear superiority in exploiting economies of scale and providing better value for money. This could be seen in the Australian market: a 30 horsepower, six cylinder, five-seater car from the United States sold, despite imperial preference, for about the same price as a small, utility, British, 10 horsepower, four cylinder, four-seater (see Table 3.1). The preference for American cars was shown in August 1947 when sterling was made convertible. Demand for British cars decreased immediately. One million pounds worth of export orders for Nuffield alone were cancelled. When convertibility of the pound was suspended the SMMT commented, 'Many countries will presumably not be able to buy as many cars as previously . . . Such conditions should confer an advantage next year [1948] on British over USA car exporters and perhaps in some cases neutralise the price differential.'[4] Obviously the SMMT, if not the government, was well aware of American productive superiority.

It was against a background of curtailed United States supply that Britain became the world's leading car exporter in 1948, replacing the United States. There a steel shortage had severely limited car exports, and as a result of that steel shortage the United States itself became a major British market along with Australia, New Zealand and South Africa. The extent of excess demand that year in the United States was put into perspective by figures released by Ford (US). At a time when total UK production was less than half a million units per year Ford (US) had orders for 1,700,000 cars but could produce only one million. Therefore the UK's position as the world's number one exporter in 1948 was the result of unusual temporary circumstances. First, the steel shortage in the United States was a transient phenomenon. Secondly, the revival of the French and German industries, by 1948 and 1949 respectively, meant competition for the UK in overseas markets was strengthening. British export achievements in the immediate post-war years were largely accounted for by the lack of available substitutes in overseas markets. Success occurred not because of, but in spite of, the fact that most British designs were inappropriate for many overseas

Table 3.1: Retail Prices of Cars in Australia, 1948 (£A)

	British Cars		
Type	Horse Power	No. of Cyls	Price (£A)
Standard	8	4	550
Riley	12	4	1,269
Vauxhall 'Wyvern'	12	4	540*
Vauxhall 'Senior'	14	6	609*
Standard	14	4	720
Wolseley	18	6	1,073
	United States or Canadian Cars		
Type	Horse Power	No. of Cyls	Price (£A)
Ford	33	8	668
Chevrolet 'Skymaster'	29	6	661
Chevrolet 'Fleetmaster'	29	6	682
Buick	30	8	1,011
Plymouth	25	6	743
Pontiac	30	6	796

*Imported in knock-down form

road and weather conditions.

Effects on Structure

Government export policy had a profound effect on the structure of
the UK motor industry. In effect, it supported the weak and outdated
manufacturers at the expense of the more efficient. To understand this
it is necessary to note the following. After World War II, existing British
production plants were too small to fully exploit available economies of
scale, as discussed in Chapter 2. Inadequate steel supplies meant that
even these less than optimal plants operated with excess capacity. Excess
demand at home and abroad meant that all producers could sell their
output somewhere; even if firms such as Singer and Standard offered less
value for money, they could still sell all they produced. Consequently,
excess demand in combination with the steel quotas made it difficult for
the largest or most efficient firms to exploit their potential superiority
and increase market shares through expansion and merger. And whilst
steel was supposed to be distributed to the firms only if they met export
quotas, in fact, some smaller less efficient firms received their steel
quotas even when they failed to meet their export quotas.[5] The steel
quotas system, in striving to be fair, effectively froze industry structure.

Most clearly, government export policy frustrated the forces of the market from operating to achieve a needed rationalisation and standardisation of the industry in order that potential economies of scale might be exploited and the international competitiveness of the industry strengthened.

Ironically, the government seemed unaware of the stranglehold their export policy had placed on industry structure. Not only had they forced the motor manufacturers to export but, since 1947, they had also stressed the export of the capital goods which a rationalisation, standardisation and modernisation of the motor industry required in order to help the balance of payments. The government's apparent unawareness of the consequences of its export policy for rationalisation, standardisation and modernisation in the motor industry were demonstrated on several occasions. In 1946 the President of the Board of Trade stressed the need for a cheap, large, standardised British car, but did not explain how and why the producers should make it.[6] In 1947 the Minister of Supply expressed deep concern about the continued diversity in the number of models offered by the motor industry and even suggested that if the motor industry could not, the government might have to, rationalise the number of model offerings.[7] No remedy was proposed nor any action taken. A prominent member of the government party, Mr Christopher Shawcross, reflected the government's view with the following observation:

Is it not obvious that the manufacturers are intending to go back to 1939 as quickly as they can, instead of ahead to 1950, as they ought to do? The manufacturers are determined to make hay while the sun shines. They know there is enormous worldwide demand at the moment, and they think that by taking the short view, by churning out quickly models for which they have the plant, tools and equipment, they can make a big profit and take no heed of the future.[8]

Effects on Conduct

The truth of the matter was that government export policy severely constrained the manufacturers' options so that rational conduct made them appear in Shawcross's words, 'heedless of the future'. The export quotas were set on a year by year basis. The motor manufacturers believed the export drive to be a short-run affair and that the home market would soon become the major market once again, as it always had been. Given the clear superiority of American efficiency in production, the Americans' pre-war dominance of export markets, and the uncertainty of likely overseas demand in the long run, profit-motivated manufacturers in the UK would have been most unwise to overstate export opportunities for the longer term.

Against this background the manufacturers had limited choice about what sort of models they sold overseas. For the most part they sold what they could where they could. Often, outdated British designs proved inconvenient, inappropriate and unreliable, and gained a poor reputation. In 1949 the Canadian correspondent to *The Economist* summed up much overseas reaction to British cars. He said,

The product of the British motor industry, with its narrow tracks, small luggage space, and reputed inability to stand up to bad roads has been criticised to the point of monotony.[9]

The only area where they were competitive was as 'second string models', for predominantly urban driving. This poor reputation was aggravated by the lack of parts and service networks which backed up British cars: parts did not count in the export quotas of the manufacturers. The lack of service networks was implicitly explained at the 1947 Austin general meeting when the chairman noted, 'valuable export markets may remain open to them [Austin] for a few months'.[10] Obviously, stopgap sales to fill such markets, in order to meet the export quotas, did not justify the development of a full service network. One result of such short-term export policies by the motor manufacturers was that breakdowns caused by minor problems overseas could become major problems for the cars' owners when parts and services were unavailable, and so alienate the owners from future British purchases. Furthermore, all British manufacturers offered a wide model range, partly as a result of pre-war taxation and competitions legislation.[11] Since they all competed in world markets, the sales penetration of any given model in any given market was likely to be very low. Thus there was scant justification for dealers around the world to carry adequate parts for any model. Finally, it would appear that many dealers were signed up very hurriedly and without much investigation in the post-war years. Consequently, poor quality dealers became a familiar characteristic of the government-inspired British sales effort overseas.

It is interesting to compare the early post-war export efforts of Volkswagen at this stage, in view of Volkswagen's later success. In 1947 the British army was responsible for appointing Mr Heinz Nordhoff, who had worked for General Motors' German Opel division before

World War II, to head the decimated Volkswagen plant. (British manufacturers offered the plant had declared it, and the car, as worthless.)
Nordhoff, with his General Motors experience, was initially as unim-
pressed with the Volkswagen car design as the British manufacturers,
though it appears that the occupation British army held the car in high
regard. He also realised the car could only be sold abroad if it sold
despite the fact that it was German. Nordhoff also knew he had to sell
the car abroad, not only because of the lack of potential demand within
Germany, but because it had been decreed that Volkswagen could only
import essential raw materials and capital machinery if it paid for the
imports with foreign currency the company itself had earned abroad by
exporting. Nordhoff knew the only hope for survival was to provide
outstanding quality and service to offset likely resistance to the strange
design and German origin. Service before sales became the key to earning
vital foreign currency so that production could be maintained. Such an
approach stands in stark contrast to the myopic export policy the British
were encouraged to take by their government.

The evidence also contradicts Shawcross's accusation that the UK
manufacturers attempted to make big profits heedless of the future.
The manufacturers set prices for the home market subject to a number
of constraints that required prices to appróximate those that would
have occurred in competitive circumstances. First, the industry had to
beware of antagonising the government into stricter controls or even
nationalisation because of profiteering. Secondly, the industry had to
consider consumer goodwill in the future: if prices dropped considerably
when normal conditions returned consumer ill-will would be generated
about price gauging. Thirdly, the industry had to be concerned about
charges of dumping by overseas governments; this could occur if the
difference between overseas and home prices became too great. And in
fact it does not appear that prices were set very much above normal
equilibrium levels. When excess demand eventually ended in Britain,
prices were not reduced; nor did profits fall. If excessively high prices
had been set, price cuts and lower profits after 1953 would have been
expected. Relative to all industries in Britain, the motor industry's
profit performance improved after excess demand ended. Even though
this is partly explained by the fact that more cars were sold in the more
profitable home market after 1952, Table 3.2 suggests that excessive
exploitation before then had not occurred.

At home, instead of high prices, long waiting lists and black markets
were created. In overseas markets price discrimination was practised to
meet the export drive and make adequate profits. For example, when

Table 3.2: Pre-tax Profits (Loss) in the UK Motor Industry, 1945-77 (£ millions)

Fiscal Year	BMC Austin	British Leyland Morris	Standard	Rootes-Chrysler	Vauxhall	Ford
1945	.9	1.9	.3	1.5	2.1	1.4
1946	1.0	3.0	.3	(.4)	1.5	3.2
1947	1.8	2.6	.3	.6	2.0	3.9
1948	1.1	1.5	.9	1.2	2.0	5.5
1949	1.6	2.6	1.2	1.1	2.7	5.1
1950	5.2	7.1	1.3	2.8	2.7	9.7
1951	7.2	8.7	2.3	3.4	2.7	9.8
1952	5.2		1.6	3.4	5.3	9.6
1953	12.3		1.6	2.2	9.9	15.7
1954	17.9		2.2	3.5	12.4	19.0
1955	20.3		3.3	3.3	10.8	18.1
1956	11.7		.8	1.7	6.4	10.0
1957	7.8		.8*	(.6)	(2.3)	20.1
1958	21.0			3.4	1.1	24.7
1959	15.7			3.9	13.5	32.2
1960	26.9			4.4	14.1	33.7
1961	10.1			2.9	14.5	22.2
1962	4.2			(.9)	16.0	17.0
1963	15.4			(.3)	16.3	35.0
1964	21.8			(.2)	17.9	24.0
1965	50			(2.5)	17.7	8.9
1966	44			(3.4)	3.6	7.4
1967	16			(10.8)	5.7	2.6
1968		38		(3.7)	9.0	43.0
1969		40		(.7)	(1.9)	38.1
1970		4		(10.7)	(9.7)	25.2
1971		32		.4	1.8	(30.7)
1972		32		1.6	(4.3)	46.8
1973		51		3.7	(4.1)	65.4
1974		2.3		(17.7)	(18.1)	8.7
1975		(23.6)		(35.5)	(2.5)	40.8
1976		(112.4)**		(31.9)	7.4	140.2
1977		72.5		(8.2)	5.2	263.1

* Becomes part of Leyland
**For 15 months

Sources: G. Maxcy and A. Silbertson, *The Motor Industry* (Allen and Unwin, London, 1958), p. 128; D.G. Rhys, *The Motor Industry: An Economic Survey* (Butterworths, London, 1972), p. 361; Parliament (Commons), *Fourteenth Report of the Expenditure Committee, 1974-75: The Motor Vehicle Industry* (HMSO, London, 1975); *Times 1000* (Times Books, London, 1978).

the Europeans returned to volume production in the late forties, prices
were lowered there, whilst in the United States cars were always sold at
prices which barely covered marginal costs so as to be price competitive.
The manufacturers carried out logical price discrimination and it was
failure to understand this that caused the outcry in the House of Commons, typified by Shawcross's statement, over the relatively high prices
of cars in the home market.

In 1948 the first new models from Britain in over a decade appeared.
This was a long time-lag since the last introduction of new models.
Furthermore, in the post-war years the motor industry had difficulty
obtaining new capital machinery for the new models. Together, these
factors meant that the new models were likely to have more than average
teething problems. The government's export drive made it necessary to
sell the new cars overseas with the inadequate dealer networks described
above. At home, information about design flaws would have been fed
back to the manufacturers for remedial action fairly quickly. From
overseas markets such feedback trickled in slowly, and in the meantime
the reputation of UK products declined further. Additionally, since the
manufacturers expected a large home market in the future, the new
models had to be appropriate for UK conditions. It is small wonder
their overseas reception was less than enthusiastic.

Overall, the government's export drive necessitated the sale of too
many ill-suited and inadequately researched models, through inadequate
dealers, with inadequate parts and service facilities, by too many manufacturers. Inevitably the reputation of British cars declined and the long-
run demand for the British products decreased.

Effects on Performance

The export drive was also disappointing in terms of the government's
own long-term economic goals. Its main effects were on technical
efficiency, economic growth and the balance of payments. On all three
economic goals the export drive had harmful long-run effects. As noted,
the system for steel allocation froze industry structure preventing a
desirable expansion of the most efficient firms. Instead, all companies
were able to continue in production well below capacity and with plants
too small to exploit all available economies of scale: the comparison of
UK and American car prices in Australia reflects the cost penalties of
the less efficient fragmented production methods in the UK and the
wasted resources this inefficiency implied. The pursuit of efficiency and
progress in the motor industry was further hampered by the emphasis
of the export drive on 'engineering goods'; at times the motor companies

experienced difficulties and delays in obtaining new capital equipment. All of these sacrifices by the motor industry might well have been more than justified if the export drive had made a significant contribution to the balance of payments. It did not. Undoubtedly in the short run the export drive squeezed some production into export markets which could have been sold at home and, except for difficulties before devaluation in 1949, the motor industry nearly met all its annual quotas. Nevertheless, the contribution of the export drive depended upon the *additional* exports it generated. In the discussion of the distribution of cars in Britain in the post-war years that follows it is shown that few additional exports were generated. The home market in the forties could not have absorbed anything like total industry output. Even without the export drive the manufacturers would have had to export a much higher proportion of output than before the war in order to fully utilise capacity and grow. However, before examining the misleading impact of the government's distribution policy on industry estimates of home demand it is necessary to first discuss the effects of rearmament policy.

Rearmament Policy

Following the 1950 Korean crisis, the government reassessed its overall economic priorities. Top priority was now given to rearmament. In order to reallocate more resources towards defence purposes, whilst minimising the effect on the balance of payments, raw materials supplies to the motor industry were further reduced. To encourage yet more exports the government cut planned home market car sales quotas to just eighty thousand for 1951 and to sixty thousand for 1952. Rearmament also required new vehicles for the military. These service demands were spread amongst the UK motor manufacturers and all received military orders. By late 1952 inflation, exacerbated by rearmament and increased competitiveness overseas, forced the new Conservative government to modify the export quotas established for each company. Instead of setting quarterly quotas the government obtained a general undertaking which said, 'the industry has undertaken to endeavour to export not less than eighty per cent of their output of passenger cars [estimated at 450,000 per year] '. As an incentive to exports the government stated that, 'allocations of steel to the industry [would] in the future be more closely related to export performance'.[12]

Effects on Basic Conditions

The reduction in supplies of raw materials to the motor industry meant further underutilisation of capacity; consequently, unit costs increased. Unit costs also rose as production was diversified to meet the increased demand for military vehicles. As a result, the motor industry had to increase prices in overseas markets at a time when the French, German and Italian industries, rejuvenated by Marshall Aid and relatively unaffected by rearmament, were increasing car output and improving efficiency. As UK cars became relatively more expensive the potential benefits from exports which the 1949 devaluation had offered were dissipated and by 1952 the UK motor industry was having great difficulty in meeting its export undertaking.

Effects on Structure

Rearmament policy extended the effective freeze on industry structure initiated by the post-war export quotas. The government continued to allocate steel to all successful companies; a success guaranteed by excess demand at home. When it came to allocating the sixty million pounds worth of military vehicle orders rearmament required, the government's policy for the motor industry emphasised again, as with the steel quotas, the equity goal at the expense of allocative efficiency and economic growth. The policy of giving defence orders to all companies continued to help the weak at the expense of the strong. Larger companies could have produced the vehicles more efficiently. If, instead, military orders had been given to the lowest bidders the pressures of competition could have encouraged increased concentration in the industry and some sought after rationalisation.

Just as spreading defence orders at home passed over a national opportunity for industry standardisation and rationalisation, the manner in which the government implemented rearmament policy meant an opportunity for international standardisation was missed. Defence orders necessitated some sacrifice of exports by the British motor industry because of the raw materials constraint. At the same time, both Germany and Italy had excess capacity as a result of the Marshall Aid rebuilding programme. It was therefore suggested that either Germany or Italy should supply either parts or vehicles to satisfy British defence requirements. NATO requirements had made the different NATO partners agree to the standardisation of planes. Similar co-operation might have been developed in the production of motor vehicles. Ministry of Defence agents went so far as to examine Fiat vehicles for their requirements. However, they could not persuade the Italians to change their specifications to British ones, nor could they obtain guarantees that British manufacturers would supply parts for Fiat vehicles. Hence rearmament policy failed to take advantage of opportunities for the rationalisation of national and international industry structure. Instead, the old UK motor industry structure with too many manufacturers, too many models and too high costs, was encouraged to continue.

Effects on Conduct

After World War II the UK motor industry had made a more rapid reconversion than its European counterparts. This had given the UK a headstart in car production. Rearmament was a major factor in the loss of the advantages of that headstart. Betweeen 1950 and 1952 the UK motor industry had to cut back on production causing an increase in costs and a slowdown in the development of new models. At the same time France and Germany made a rapid advance. By 1952 Volkswagens and small Renaults were being produced in greater volumes than any UK model. At the beginning of 1950 the UK had been producing over ten thousand cars per week; by the middle of 1952 weekly production was below nine thousand. In comparison, at the beginning of 1950, France and Germany combined produced eight thousand cars per week; by the middle of 1952 they produced over 13,000 per week. In 1950 the UK had exported one half of exports to the sterling area; by 1952 nearly three-quarters were sent there. In free markets such as Holland and Switzerland UK cars had clearly become too expensive.

One important additional explanation for the reduction in international competitiveness of the British motor industry during rearmament was the lower levels of industry concentration when compared to Germany, France and Italy. Another explanation was the wide range of models, to some extent a consequence of pre-war taxation and competitions policies, produced by the UK's six mass manufacturers at this time. All, except Vauxhall who did not produce a small car, attempted to produce a complete range of cars from small to large. In comparison, in Germany Volkswagen concentrated on small cars, Mercedes-Benz on larger luxury cars. Opel and Ford produced medium sized cars. In France Citroën produced very small and luxury cars. Renault produced small and medium cars. Panhard produced small cars. Simca produced medium cars. Peugeot produced medium and larger cars. In Italy Fiat dominated the market.

Without doubt the existence of an apparently huge demand at home for cars had encouraged the UK manufacturers to see the export market as a stopgap one and the home market as their long-term area of interest. By the time rearmament was completed in 1952 there were over one million domestic orders for new cars. Late in the year the steel shortage was declared over and the export quotas, which had already been reduced earlier in the face of export difficulties, were abandoned. At last the industry was ready and able to exploit the enormous home market. It turned out to be a mirage. Despite thirteen years of severely restricted home sales, real excess demand turned out to be extremely limited. In total in 1952 less than 100,000 cars over the original stingy 60,000 home quota were sold. Still, by October 1952, second-hand car prices were falling rapidly. Many offers to deliver cars to people on waiting lists were rejected. By November some cars were available for immediate delivery. Before the end of the year the chairman of Austin appealed for cuts in purchase tax on cars in order to stave off redundancy. The myth about enormous pent-up demand at home for cars had been shattered.

Hindsight makes it easy to understand this hopeless overestimate of home demand. First, there was no precedent for the motor industry of a long-sustained restriction of supply such as occurred in the forties; therefore, demand estimates were highly unreliable and of little help. Secondly, there was a conflict between the usage age of the car stock and the historic age. Historically the stock of cars was old. However, for many years most of the cars had been unused. Furthermore, designs had been little changed for over ten years. The manufacturers anticipated that the stock of 'old' cars needed replacing but in fact many of these cars had been little used and were, in terms of usage, quite 'new'.

Effects on Performance

With rearmament policy the government required the motor industry to contribute to the government's overall goals by making a bigger short-term effort to help the balance of payments, and by providing essential military vehicles. These goals were achieved but at a considerable and, as the discussion of distribution policy below reveals, unnecessary cost. Briefly, the costs of rearmament policy in terms of overall economic objectives were:

(i)   It continued to discourage the much needed rationalisation of the motor industry, already hindered by five years of export quotas, so detracting from allocative efficiency.
(ii) Research and design were redirected towards military vehicles.
(iii) Steel quotas and military orders held up economic growth in the industry for two more years.
(iv) Long-run export efforts, such as those forced upon Volkswagen, were discouraged as the home waiting lists became artificially inflated by distribution policy.

Distribution Policy

The problem of distributing inadequate supplies of cars for the home market between 1945 and 1952 was left to the industry, the government only specifying that 'essential demand' at home had priority. 'Essential demand' applied mainly to people with occupations which required a car in the social interest, for example, doctors and district nurses.

Responsibility for allocating cars after 1945 fell to the British Motor Traders Association (BMTA). Anybody who wanted a car had to put their name on a waiting list, unless part of 'essential demand'. When their name came to the top of the list they received a car at the current retail price. The BMTA made new car buyers sign a covenant under which they agreed not to sell the car for at least one year, but since it was not legally binding it was often ignored and cars sold at highly inflated prices. For instance, some doctors, who were given immediate delivery, made handsome profits from the scheme. By 1950 public consternation over this sort of abuse was sufficient to make the BMTA instruct their members not to sell cars to people who already had cars in good condition; but as there were no records of who had had new cars or who currently owned them available to retailers, the 1950 instruction was easily circumvented. Only in 1952 was a false declaration about ownership of post-war vehicles made grounds for legal action, and by then excess demand was just about at an end.

Not only were cars scarce after the war but so was petrol to run them. In June 1945 the government introduced petrol rationing. Before that no petrol had been available to ordinary citizens. Initially, every car was provided with a monthly ration sufficient to travel one hundred and fifty miles. Twice in 1946 the ration was slightly raised. Following the 1947 energy crisis and balance of payments difficulties it was totally withdrawn. Then in June 1948 it was renewed at eighty miles per month and a year later doubled. In May 1950 it was abandoned, but because Britain still faced balance of payments difficulties petrol imports had to be curbed somehow. For some time it had been argued that motoring was a middle-class luxury and that, therefore, higher prices would make more efficient use of scarce petrol than rationing.[13] The Labour government appeared to accept these arguments and doubled the petrol tax from ninepence to one shilling and sixpence.

Effects on Basic Conditions

Excess demand in the home market meant a sellers market and the manufacturers could sell just about any make or model. For example, in 1951 Nuffield had to ship back from the United States a number of Morris cars it had been unable to sell. The cars were overhauled, reconditioned, converted to right-hand drive and then sold for a price which included all these additional costs including the shipping. Such easy sales undoubtedly encouraged the manufacturers to believe the huge overestimates of excess demand in Britain fostered by the BMTA's distribution system. Given that the second-hand price of a nearly new car was sometimes double its list price, the BMTA's system of distribution encouraged everybody who vaguely hoped to be able to pay for a new car to put their name on the waiting list. No deposit was required when a car was ordered. Therefore, if one's turn came up and the car was not wanted, either it could be refused, or it could be briefly held and then sold for a considerable profit. In addition, people could put their name on more than one maker's list. Looking back, it is apparent that the waiting list was a poor indicator of the extent of excess demand. Nevertheless, manufacturers used the waiting list as evidence that a huge pent-up demand for cars existed in Britain. At the time this seemed reasonable. New car sales in Britain had been heavily curtailed since 1939 so that the existing stock of cars had a high average age. Consequently, it was reasonable to believe it largely needed replacement.

Effects on Structure

The post-war sellers market in Britain removed much of the incentive for manufacturers to be efficient. There was little pressure to rationalise domestic sales networks or provide superior parts and service. Prices were set at levels which were not so high as to generate government interference on the grounds of profiteering. Then, manufacturers sold cars to a public grateful for anything it could get, in the extreme case converted rejects from the United States. As a result there was little pressure to emphasise quality.

Effects on Conduct

Usually petrol rationing will cause a decrease in car demand. Between 1945 and 1950 it is likely that excess demand for cars would have been greater still if adequate supplies of petrol had been available. The important effect of petrol rationing, however, was on designs. The government allocated to every car sufficient petrol for a given *mileage*. The main purpose of this was to encourage the acceptance of larger cars in the home market. The government felt Britain should produce larger American-sized cars in order to be competitive in export markets. One consequence was that none of the small post-war British designs, such as the Morris Minor or Austin Dorset, were as economical as the small French Renault 750, the German Volkswagen or the Italian Fiat 500. At the same time the failure of other government policies to effect rationalisation and cost efficiencies in the motor industry meant that the larger British cars were considerably more expensive than similar American designs in overseas markets and not therefore competitive. In fact the government had misread the situation, as Volkswagen's later export success demonstrated. American overseas market domination was not the result of large-sized models so much as of reliable, good-value-for-money products.

Effects on Performance

Distribution policy had undesirable consequences for the motor industry. Most importantly it created an illusion of huge excess demand: this reduced the incentive to rationalise production and marketing methods to lower costs and improve quality. In addition, the petrol distribution system affected the design of cars by eliminating much of the emphasis for fuel economy; hence engine efficiency and small-car design were discouraged. And even though the manufacturers knew that competition would eventually return and therefore went ahead with new designs, progress in this sphere was not totally satisfactory. Since a rationalisation of industry had not taken place too many models were produced by too many manufacturers in too small quantities. Allocative efficiency, therefore, was not enhanced by distribution policy.

Taxation Policy

In the inter-war years the domestic car market had been protected not only by the McKenna import duties, levied at a hefty $33\frac{1}{3}$ per cent, but also by the method by which cars were taxed. Cars were taxed in proportion to their RAC horsepower.[14] This tax encouraged the design of what are called long-stroke engines. These engines were unsuitable for high-speed, long-distance travel, such as was more common overseas, because the long-stroke engine implied long movements by the engine pistons and hence additional stress at high speed. The tax also meant that most imported cars, typically of more efficient, shorter stroke design, were overtaxed in Britain in relation to their power output as compared to similar domestic cars. Hence the tax had discouraged both car exports and car imports up to 1939. If the British motor industry was to be successful after the war in overseas markets and was to build appropriately designed cars, a revision of the tax system was essential.

Initially the government decided that after January 1947 cars would have an engine capacity tax of one pound per hundred cubic centimetres, with a minimum of seven pounds and ten shillings, levied upon them. This engine cubic capacity tax would have been protective both against large-engined American cars and very small-engined cars such as the Italian Fiat 500, whilst giving much more freedom to engine design than the RAC tax. However, by 1947 worldwide excess demand had become apparent and the threat of American imports to Britain had disappeared.[15] Furthermore the costs of car ownership in Britain relative to average incomes had increased since 1939 so that a further change in taxation policy seemed desirable to lower the costs of a new car and encourage new car demand in the long run. It was decided that all new cars registered after 1947 would pay a flat rate licence duty of ten pounds per annum. Prior to the change all but the smallest cars had paid over ten pounds in licence duties, so to help offset revenue losses the government stipulated that all older cars first registered before 1947 would continue to pay the old horsepower tax and the purchase tax on the small minority of new cars with a base price of over one thousand pounds would be doubled to $66\frac{2}{3}$ per cent.[16]

Consequences of Taxation Policy

Clearly, both tax system changes introduced after the war sought to affect the nature of car demand in accordance with the best interests of the motor industry. The cubic capacity tax was intended to make British cars more acceptable in overseas markets without opening up the UK market to the Americans. The flat rate licence system sought to modify British designs towards those larger designs which the government believed, at the time, would sell more easily overseas. A further aim of the tax changes was to affect industry structure by encouraging the manufacturers, particularly the larger ones, to reduce their model range and so exploit economies of scale and lower unit costs.

The flat rate tax successfully encouraged the development of larger, less stressed, less economical engines. Yet the new larger UK models of the late forties were received no more enthusiastically overseas than their predecessors. Despite considerably higher wages the Americans, because of a more efficient industry structure which exploited economies of scale, achieved lower per unit costs and were able to provide better value for money. (In 1935 the USA had produced 15 times as many cars as the UK with twice the labour force.[17]) At the same time, in Europe, the smallest and cheapest cars which ironically Britain had successfully produced before the war, with models such as the Austin Seven, sold best. This was because, in part, relatively few pre-war cars had survived the war there to provide cheap basic motoring. Consequently, the marginal buyer had to turn to the new car market for less expensive private transportation. The option available in Britain of a second-hand car, albeit overpriced, to provide cheaper private transportation was not so available in Europe. In Europe, the larger, less spartan UK cars offered too much and were too expensive to buy and to operate to compete with models such as the basic Renaults, Volkswagens and Fiats.

The effect of taxation policy on structure was limited. Taxation changes were a necessary but not sufficient condition for the rationalisation of industry structure. The changes in taxation took place in the vacuum created by the government's export policies. Since all firms made adequate profits between 1945 and 1953 there was little incentive for firms, many of which were controlled by individual families and trusts, to give way to merger and takeover movements. Consequently the intended aim of taxation reform, to reduce the number of models offered by a more concentrated industry, did not take place to the desired extent.

Looking back, it is clear that the way in which the government altered taxation policies after the war did encourage the production of larger models and reduced the emphasis on economy models, as intended. But the government had misread the situation. In Europe, small economy cars were in greatest demand by the end of the forties. Where large cars were in demand the UK cars were too expensive, relative to American cars, because of the failure of the UK industry to exploit economies of scale. Thus the performance goal, to stimulate exports and help the balance of payments was not satisfactorily achieved by taxation policy.

Finally, the post-war Labour government placed considerable emphasis on the overall goal of equity. It would appear that the application of the flat rate tax system was inequitous since the owners of older cars were taxed under the old RAC method and paid higher taxes. The lower flat rate system only applied to newer cars. In 1947 it was doubtful whether the Chancellor of the Exchequer felt the implementation of the tax change was regressive. Until the 1950s any motor car was regarded as a luxury of the middle class. At that time, therefore, almost all car taxes, even on older cars, were paid by upper income groups.

Roads and Transport Policy

Between 1939 and 1945 the government exercised considerable control over transport in Britain. The 1947 Transport Act continued this control with the nationalisation of the railways, long-distance road haulage, some road passenger vehicles, inland waterways and London City Transport.

The intention of the 1947 Act was to integrate all forms of transport under a British Transport Commission, which became the largest employer of labour in Britain.

The rapid growth of passenger and freight road transport in the 1950s and the decline of the railways was not foreseen when the 1947 Act was drawn up. Road expenditures, of which the majority came from the central government, reflected this. Pre-war road expenditures had been niggardly in comparison to revenues. Post-war governments continued the trend (see Figure 3.1). In May the Labour government announced a new road programme aimed at promoting road safety, increasing agricultural efficiency, improving industrial and urban development, and reducing road congestion. However, before the programme was even begun, balance of payments difficulties caused a reduction in government expenditures. The roads were an obvious candidate for postponement. From 1948 to 1953 roads policy was one of 'patch and mend'. Even compared to pre-war levels roads expenditures were low. Between 1948 and 1953 only 66 per cent of the amounts spent between 1936 and 1938 were made on minor improvements and maintenance, and only 21 per cent of the amount on major improvements and new construction. Yet as late as 1952 the Treasury held the viewpoint that so long as expenditures by the Ministry of Transport remained below three-quarters of the 1938 expenditures no extravagant expenditures were taking place.[18]

Consequences of Road and Transport Policy

The nature of a country's road system can itself affect the motor industry. It is thought to affect motor industry performance in two important ways. The first relates to the question of a saturation point for motor car demand. The second relates to the nature of motor car design.

The idea of a saturation point has been popular for a long time. By this argument, the total demand for cars is eventually a function of the road network. At some point congestion on the roads will become so bad that a constraint is put on further motor car ownership. The costs of congestion outweigh the benefits, for aspiring motorists, of car ownership. Although this argument was to be raised again in the late 1950s, between 1945 and 1953 the government, by artificially keeping down the number of cars on the road and the number of miles they were driven, obviated the likelihood of a saturation point in demand ever appearing even a possibility.

The second concept, the relationship between the nature of the roads

Figure 3.1: Annual Expenditures on Road Construction, Improvement and Maintenance, 1945-77

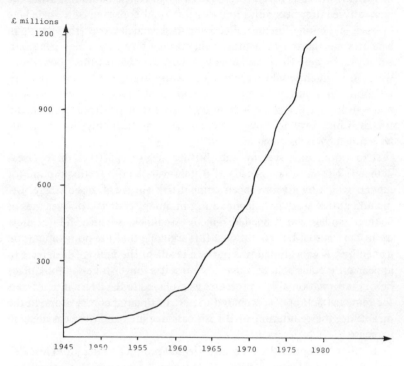

Source: Central Statistical Office.

and car design, was highly relevant between 1945 and 1953. Different road classification systems in different countries complicate a direct comparison between British roads and those of other countries in the post-war years. However, United States roads were excellent because the law dictated that road expenditures increased proportionately with motor tax revenues. In Germany, Hitler had built the famous autobahns. In France, dating from Napoleonic times, there was a national main trunk system, with long straight roads relatively free of obstacles. In Britain, the roads tended to follow the rights of way determined by medieval institutions.

The neglect of the road system had an important impact on British car demand. To understand this it is helpful to imagine, for example, the state of the main A1 road from London to the North and Scotland in the post-war years. First, the A1 bypassed few of the major connurbations in its path. Thus, the main street of Newcastle, the seventh largest city in Britain, was also part of the A1. Through traffic could not avoid the busy city centre. Secondly, most of this road consisted of a single lane in each direction. Finally, all commercial vehicles over three tons in weight were limited to a maximum speed of twenty miles per hour. British roads were slow and congested. Cars suitable for these conditions were ones which would trundle along easily in top gear at twenty miles per hour with sufficient engine torque to accelerate to forty or fifty miles an hour when the opportunity to pass slow traffic arose. Demand for such high-revving, low-geared cars was, quite simply, incompatible with much overseas demand.

The poor road system had further negative effects on overseas demand. The antiquated roads of Britain were a poor testing ground for models which might have been competitive abroad. Consequently, UK manufacturers were handicapped in obtaining feedback on weaknesses in their models which needed remedy; weaknesses which did not show up in the unusual UK conditions. It is arguable that the poor reputation gained by UK cars abroad was partly a result of the failure for defects to appear on models sold at home. As a result a longer time-lag took place before information about problems was relayed to the UK manufacturers for remedial action, as compared to her continental competitors. In the meantime, the reputation of British cars declined and overseas demand decreased.

In summary, poor British roads affected product strategy and research and innovation. Designs were created which were suitable mainly for British conditions. Research was directed towards the problems created by British roads. Thus British cars tended to emphasise manoeuvrability, light steering and good engine torque and to de-emphasise high-speed cruising ability. Furthermore, poor roads slowed progress in the industry by retarding the development of the technology appropriate to models suitable for a modern road system, such as those found overseas.

Labour Relations Policy

No discussion of the British motor industry in the post-war years can neglect labour relations in the industry. Frequently, the poor performance of the British motor industry since World War II has been blamed on troublesome labour relations. Yet in the first two decades after the war the government labour policy, with reference to the motor industry, was mainly one of setting the ground rules. Unless the industrial democratic process broke down the government did not get involved in day-to-day problems. For instance, in 1947 most of the motor industry moved to a five-day week from a five-and-a-half day week. At the same time the Trades Union Congress (TUC) moved that a forty-hour week should be introduced in the industry. When the unions asked the Labour government to take action on this motion, the government replied that it was a matter for negotiation not legislation. In other words both political parties supported free collective bargaining in the post-war era. Nevertheless, government labour policy did influence the industry. First, wartime legislation, which had allowed trade unions in the motor plants, had changed the ground rules considerably. Secondly, when labour relations broke down the government set up courts of inquiry which examined problems, made recommendations and set precedents.

Whilst there were a number of strikes between 1945 and 1953, there was only one occasion on which a court of inquiry was established. The question involved in the 'McHugh' strike was whether Austin had victimised a shop steward called McHugh. McHugh was one of a number of workers declared redundant. Set up by the Minister of Labour, the court concluded that McHugh's dismissal,

> was neither selective nor irregular in form and cannot be attributed to victimisation on account of . . . trade union activities. Furthermore [the strike] was not based upon any real grievance as to [McHugh's] dismissal or the form which it had taken, but was designed by [the Area Organiser of the National Union of Vehicle Builders] to secure the principle of preferential treatment for shop stewards . . .[19]

The court of inquiry ruled that shop stewards should not get preferential treatment.

Consequences of Labour Relations Policy

Before the war the motor industry had had a reputation for hire-and-fire practices. As a result of wartime legislation trade unions had been introduced into all previously non-unionised factories, sometimes under duress, and in all cases the motor firms had been encouraged to allow many different unions into the factories. As a consequence of there being many unions, shop stewards played an important role at the shop floor level in co-ordinating the activities of the workers. The fact that in some cases unions had been forcibly introduced created scope for management-labour antagonism. The fact that shop stewards, rather than local union officials, really represented the shop floor created scope for shop steward/union official jealousies and antagonism. In an industry particularly vulnerable to seasonal and cyclical demand, such a labour relations system, to a considerable extent a consequence of wartime government policy, was likely to be unsatisfactory and controversial, as events proved. One instance occurred as early as 1947. At the Morris Motors Annual General Meeting, Sir Miles Thomas, the managing director, reported that 'extravagant expansions' had been cancelled because of labour difficulties. However, other factors, such as reduced steel supplies, fuel shortages, a lack of access to capital goods, the coldest winter for many years and the uncertainty of demand overseas must also have discouraged expansion. Poor labour relations became in this case, as in others, simply a convenient justification, or even scapegoat, for actions which resulted from a number of related and unrelated factors.

More clearly, the poor labour relations system had a negative effect on the cost structure of the industry. Distrust and insecurity meant that labour relations in the motor industry became characterised by a rigid adherence to demarcation, petty jealousies, and a reluctance to permit the introduction of new technology and labour-saving machinery. British trade unions tended to oppose moves for modernisation and improved efficiency which might possibly have involved the elimination of jobs. An example of this was a case at Austin in 1948 which ended in a strike that closed down the factory. Austin wanted to introduce a new spindle cutter which had the ability to increase productivity by 140 per cent. Shop stewards feared the new machine would result in a 'speed up' with possible adverse effects on jobs. Therefore, they opposed the introduction of the new machine.

The same Austin strike reflected another negative aspect of a poor labour relations system on costs. This developed out of the piecework systems. Under piecework the worker was paid for each unit he produced. The faster he was able to produce, the more he got paid. The difficulty with such a system was that it made innovation difficult and expensive. First, if, as was the case with Austin's spindle cutter, the worker could no longer control his rate of output with a new machine it was likely there would be resistance to change. Secondly, a new machine applicable to piecework would only be accepted if it was likely to generate higher wages than the old machine. At Austin the strike was aggravated by difficulties in setting a new wage rate for the spindle cutters. The problem was that once one group got a new rate for the job, parity meant demands by other groups for wage increases. With over twenty unions to a plant the scope for conflict and increased pressures on costs was considerable. It is interesting to note that as early as 1948 these sorts of difficulties persuaded Standard-Triumph

International (STI) to buy out their piecework system with large wage increases which meant STI paid the highest wages in the industry. It is also interesting to note that in the 1950s the unions pressured STI to reintroduce piecework.

There were several consequences of the unsatisfactory fragmented labour relations system on motor industry conduct and performance. First, it meant considerable resources and effort were wasted on labour relations problems which might better have been applied elsewhere. Secondly, poor labour relations tended to discourage research and innovation. Every time new methods and techniques were introduced into production they created a hazard for labour relations, and therefore the innovation of new research was slowed. (To some extent the hostility and defensive attitudes of the unions which led to strikes and demarcation can be traced back to pre-war days when firms such as Ford had violently opposed trade unions.) Thirdly, the existence and attitudes of the unions affected employment stability in the industry. The existence of unions meant the firms had to make greater efforts to avoid redundancies than before the war, so encouraging better production planning but also labour hoarding in times of weak demand. Finally, the labour relations system as it existed after the war had negative effects on the balance of payments: whenever the system broke down and strikes occurred exports were lost.

Whilst strikes do not necessarily indicate a poor labour relations system, the number of strikes in the British motor industry after 1945 suggests weaknesses. One of the major weaknesses stemmed from the way in which government legislation during the war had permitted trade unions in the factories. It had given no incentive to a rational trade union structure such as one union to each plant and such, ironically, as Allied Command introduced in West Germany and played an important role in the stable labour relations that enabled that country's motor industry to achieve great post-war success. Instead, in Britain, far too many unions were present in each plant for efficient labour relations.

Competitions Policy

In Britain the attitude to monopoly *per se* has been less critical than in other countries, notably the United States which has a long history of anti-monopoly legislation. In Britain, in general, monopolies have been accepted unless they performed unsatisfactorily. Indeed it was not until 1948 that any monopoly control legislation was passed and the 1948 Monopolies and Restrictive Practices Act was pretty tame legislation when compared to United States laws. Under the Act the Board of Trade

could refer individual industrial arrangements to a Monopolies Commission for examination.

As for the motor industry, the post-war government favoured greater
industry concentration so that economies of scale might be exploited.
With profound, insight the Minister of Supply in 1946 said the motor
industry would commit 'general suicide' if rationalisation did not occur,
and the government went so far as to encourage co-operation and collusion between the independent firms believing this would lead to
mergers and increased efficiency. It was as a government achievement
that the Minister of Supply announced that the 'big six' had agreed to
pool the results of production experiments and to allow the other
manufacturers to inspect the technical and administrative resources
of its rivals. Government encouragement for inter-firm collusion was
further shown in its acknowledgement and intercourse with the SMMT,
in the setting up of a National Advisory Committee on the Motor
Industry in 1946, and its general support of other intra-industry bodies
such as the BMTA.

Consequences of Competitions Policy

Though the government clearly favoured the rationalisation and integration of the motor firms, other government policies, as shown, thwarted
the achievement of this goal. As a result relatively few mergers occurred
between 1945 and 1953. The only really important one, which mainly
affected industry structure, was between Austin and Morris in 1952. In
addition to the Austin-Morris merger, a number of takeovers of body
suppliers took place. In 1946 Austin absorbed Vanden Plas. In 1947
the British Small Arms Company (Daimler) purchased Hooper (coach
builders) and Barker (coach builders). In 1953 Ford bought out Briggs,
and BMC took over Fisher and Ludlow. In 1954 BSA took control of
Carbodies.

The background to the 1952 Austin-Morris merger was as follows.
Since before World War II the two American companies, Ford and Vauxhall, had taken an increasing share of the British market. At the end of
1948 plans for technical collaboration were made between Austin and
Morris. The move was spurred on by current difficulties in meeting export
quotas. In 1949, following devaluation, the profits of both Austin and
Morris more than trebled. Consequently, neither company felt the need
to sacrifice any autonomy. The merger was called off. In 1951 the
austerity created by rearmament put pressure on both companies again.
In November 1951 the desire 'to effect the maximum standardisation,
coupled with the most efficient manufacture, and by the pooling of

factory resources and consequent reduction in costs'[20] led to a complete merger. The government saw the Austin-Morris merger to be in the public interest for two reasons. First, potential production economies of scale created the opportunity to lower costs. Secondly, the merger strengthened the purely British sector of the industry in relation to Ford and Vauxhall. The managing director of the new British Motor Company (BMC), Leonard Lord, saw the merger as a defensive one against the American companies. Commenting on the merger, he said, 'we expect keen competition, but we have a few shillings in the bank and friends who will lend us money. We are feeling pretty comfortable.'[21]

The two companies involved were approximately the same size in terms of output. However, Nuffield, whose market share had declined since 1937, was comprised of a number of manufacturing companies accumulated over the years. The largest of these was Morris Motors at Cowley. In addition, there was MG at Abingdon, Wolseley at Birmingham, Riley at Coventry and Morris Commercials at Birmingham. Component parts manufacturers in the Nuffield group were Nuffield Metal Products (body builders) and SU carburettors. In contrast to the fragmented Nuffield operation Austin was highly integrated with a single large plant at Longbridge which, Austin claimed, was as advanced as any in Europe. At the time of the merger, BMC produced thirteen different engines and twenty-three different body styles. To be effective in exploiting potential economies of scale the new company required a considerable reorganisation: a reorganisation that was never truly effected.

In 1953 two of the largest independent body suppliers were taken over by the motor manufacturers. Ford purchased Briggs body suppliers and BMC absorbed Fisher and Ludlow. Neither move was opposed by the government which believed the vertical integration of the firms would improve efficiency. Indeed, the fact that the Treasury allowed Ford scarce American dollars to purchase 62 per cent of Briggs's shares from the American parent company and other American interests, reflected a very strong government inclination to that merger.

A number of factors led to the Ford takeover of Briggs. First, there had been considerable labour problems at Briggs, traceable in large measure to the number of unions representing labour there and introduced as a result of wartime legislation. Ford believed that these problems would be eased by a closer integration between Ford's Dagenham works and their adjoining body suppliers. Secondly, in 1953 excess demand for cars in Britain came to an end. As competition at home and abroad became more intense all the manufacturers became more concerned about guaranteeing their supplies. Thirdly, after the war the manufacturers introduced designs featuring unitary body construction: with unitary construction a single chassis body unit replaces a separate chassis to which a body is affixed and so enables considerable weight savings. This meant the body became a more important part of the car.

Much the same factors leading to the Ford merger explained the BMC takeover of Fisher and Ludlow. Although not plagued by labour problems to the same extent, BMC's newest designs were of unitary construction. In addition, BMC wished to guarantee their supplies of this major item.

The intention of government mergers policy in this period was to encourage industry rationalisation and a reduction in the number of models produced. However, a lenient attitude towards monopolies was a necessary but not sufficient condition to achieve a satisfactory model range. Between 1945 and 1953 a single merger occurred and this did not lead to a satisfactory model range since BMC continued to try to meet every segment of the market with a wide range of models. Consequently, the overall effect of competitions policy on conduct during this period was fairly limited.

As a note of interest, the government permitted the BMC-Fisher and Ludlow merger only upon assurances that 'future trading will be materially unchanged' and that 'all enquiries and orders (whether from the motor industry or not) will receive the same attention as before'.[22] Before the merger Fisher and Ludlow had supplied bodies to STI. Hence, after the merger BMC supplied bodies to one of its major competitors.

Summary

Between 1945 and 1953 a number of government policies exerted a considerable influence, sometimes as intended, sometimes not, on the UK motor industry. The intent of the export quotas was to redirect output to overseas markets, first to help the balance of payments and later to help rearmament. To the extent that far more cars were exported after the war than before, that considerable foreign earnings resulted, and that rearmament requirements were fulfilled, the government's export policy must be deemed successful. Nevertheless, the costs involved were considerable and largely unanticipated. The intent of the distribution policy was to achieve a fair distribution of scarce cars and petrol at home. Together the export quotas and distribution policy had unintended harmful effects on the industry and economy. A necessary rationalisation of the industry was frustrated. Car designs were modified, mistakenly if intentionally, so that they proved, unintentionally, inappropriate for overseas market conditions. Perhaps most importantly the export quotas and distribution policy created, unintentionally, an illusion of enormous pent-up demand at home. This acted as a disincentive to the development of overseas markets by the manufacturers. Inadequate road expenditures and a flat rate system of taxation also pressured the British manufacturers to produce designs inappropriate for many overseas markets. Together export quotas and rearmament policy thwarted the intentions of favourable monopolies regulations to stimulate much rationalisation of the British motor industry. In addition, constant problems were created by a labour relations system, set up largely as a result of government wartime legislation, which was incapable of handling the problems of a complex modern industry. Consequently, whatever the weaknesses of British labour and management during this period, government policies between 1945 and 1953 created an environment which in many situations could only frustrate the better intentions of both labour and management.

Notes

1. HCD, 11 Apr. 1949, col. 2449.
2. Ibid., 5 Apr. 1946, col. 1584.
3. Ibid.
4. Society of Motor Manufacturers and Traders, *The Motor Industry of Great Britain*, 1947.
5. One reason why the government did not force the closure of small companies that failed to export was that some countries, for instance Argentina, only allowed imports of UK cars if the importer held a certain minimum amount of sterling in Buenos Aires. External policies such as this were felt to discriminate against the small producer. Another reason was that some of the smaller companies, for instance Allard and Healey, enjoyed great success at this time in international car rallies and, argued the SMMT, brought international prestige to Britain even if they did not meet the export quotas.
6. HCD, 5 Apr. 1946, col. 1584.
7. Ibid., 7 July 1947, col. 196.
8. Ibid., 5 Apr. 1946, col. 1584.
9. *The Economist*, Oct. 1949, p. 627.
10. Austin Motor Company, *Annual Report*, 1947.
11. See p. 43.
12. HCD, 10 June 1952, col. 135.
13. W. Plowden, *The Motor Car and Politics, 1896-1970* (The Bodley Head, London, 1971), p. 318.
14. The RAC horsepower was determined by the area of the engine piston heads.
15. See p. 34.

16. Plowden, *Motor Car and Politics*, p. 313.

17. HCD, 5 Apr. 1946, col. 1584.

18. T.C. Barker and C.I. Savage, *An Economic History of Transport in Britain* (Hutchison, London, 1974), p. 232.

19. H.A. Turner, G. Clark and G. Roberts, *Labour Relations in the Motor Industry* (Allen and Unwin, London, 1967), p. 273.

20. *The Times*, 12 Oct. 1948.

21. *Financial Times*, 28 Sept. 1954.

22. *The Economist*, 8 Aug. 1953, p. 410.

4 MODEST PROGRESS, 1953-59

With the end of rearmament, the new Conservative government reverted to more traditional *laissez faire* policies. Essentially it was thought the government should avoid interfering in industry. Consequently export quotas and steel quotas for the motor industry were abandoned and the motor industry was left to act in its own best interests. As a result the industry abandoned the emphasis on exports forced upon it since 1946. Instead, attention was paid to replacing the outdated stock of cars on British roads and making new sales at home. Between 1951 and 1955 home sales grew annually by 38 per cent. At the same time exports stagnated and did not even achieve the levels of 1951.

Regulatory Policy

Although the Conservative government followed a general 'hands off' approach towards the economy, its regulatory policy had a considerable impact on the UK motor industry. Government regulatory policy after 1953 became caricatured as 'stop-go' policy. The need for such a policy resulted from Britain's high marginal propensity to import, an over-valued pound at a fixed exchange rate, and the consequently vulnerable nature of the British balance of payments. Whenever the British economy experienced economic growth, imports tended to grow faster than exports. As a result the balance of payments tended to move into deficit. To remedy the balance of payments the government introduced restrictive measures on the internal economy until the balance of payments improved. Thus, the economy tended to follow a stop-go pattern.

The motor industry was probably affected more by stop-go policies than any other industry in Britain. First, as the country's major exporting industry, any decline in motor exports had a noticeably harmful effect on the balance of payments. Secondly, whenever it was necessary to improve the balance of payments, the government would reduce internal demand. Consumer durable demand, particularly demand for cars, was very susceptible to general restrictions. Hence the motor industry tended to feel the brunt of the country's balance of payments difficulties from two directions.

From the end of rearmament until 1955 was a period of 'go'. Failure to export more cars, however, between 1952 and 1955 partly explained the balance of payments problem which developed in 1955 and necessitated 'stop' policies. When exports of cars to North America, Europe and Australia all declined in 1955, the government reacted by tightening credit. Hire purchase restrictions on cars were increased and the down payment raised. In addition the business allowance on cars was abolished. The intention of these moves was to cut home demand so as to squeeze more cars to the declining export market. 1956 turned out to be a 'brutally disappointing year' for the UK motor industry.[1] The industry was already suffering from the government's stop policies when the Suez crisis occurred. Suez severely affected demand. In Britain, petrol taxes were raised and petrol rationing was introduced to deal with the oil shortage, and as a result home demand for new cars plummeted. Overseas demand also decreased in the many export markets short of oil. Overall, 1956 output fell by forty per cent.

The motor industry was so badly hit by the stop policies and Suez that the government took special action to help 'for the time being'.[2] Hire purchase deposits were lowered and the Board of Trade's Export Credit Department stretched its insurance credit to British manufacturers. However, neither move helped very much. The hire purchase balance on new car sales at home still had to be repaid within two years, and since most new car sales involved the trade-in of an older model the lower deposit had minimal impact. It was an unforeseen external event that brought help and some prosperity back to the UK motor industry in 1957. North America fell in love with the small car. Demand for all European cars increased rapidly. As second cars, as students' cars and as fun cars, sales of the European products were higher than ever before. British exports to North America quadrupled, though some European manufacturers, including Volkswagen, enjoyed even larger increases. Despite the continuation of stop policies domestic demand also increased in 1957: an end to petrol rationing and a rise in consumer confidence following the end of Suez appeared to offset the effects of reimposed stiffer hire purchase requirements. By 1958 the balance of payments was considerably improved following two years of stop, and increased car exports were a contributory factor to this improvement. The government decided that the economy could be expanded. All hire purchase restrictions were removed. Home sales of cars increased rapidly. Extra capacity which had been created since 1954 in the industry was fully utilised for the first time. In 1957 output had been 860,000 units; in 1958 it just exceeded one million; in 1959 it approached 1.4 million; and still there were waiting lists of up to nine months for some models at home. Optimism swept the industry and all firms made bold expansion plans.

By the summer of 1960, the balance of payments had seriously deteriorated again. The government felt compelled to implement stop policies again. The effects on the motor industry were disastrous again. Industry output in October 1960 was less than forty per cent of the peak summer levels, with the smaller firms such as Rootes and STI particularly hard hit.[3]

The deterioration in the balance of payments in 1960 occurred for two reasons. First, an anticipated rise in imported goods of all sorts accompanied the period of economic growth from 1958. Secondly, the export of British cars to North America which had begun in 1957 came to a natural end. The increased penetration of European imports caused the North American manufacturers to develop compact cars. For 1960 the Chevrolet Corvair, the Ford Falcon, and the Chrysler Valiant were announced. Demand for British cars in the United States was more affected than demand for the other European makes. A major reason for this was British post-war taxation policy which had discouraged the production of economy cars. Most British exports were small four-door saloons, with engines of between thirteen hundred and twenty-six hundred cubic capacity, and sports cars. The British saloons were closer substitutes to the North American compacts than, for example, the French Renaults and German Volkswagens. British saloons were virtually eliminated from the North American market. Renault sales fell by only thirty per cent. Sales of the German Volkswagen were least affected though Volkswagen had to launch a major advertising campaign for the first time in order to maintain sales using the slogan 'Think Small', and emphasising how a Volkswagen offered the most basic transportation available.[4]

As usual when a recession hit the motor industry, the industry appealed to the government for relief. In 1960 the response from the Chancellor of the Exchequer was that 'the important thing as regards the motor industry and the national interest is that exports should be maintained at a high level'.[5] Credit controls and purchase tax would be eased only when the government thought that the economy as a whole justified it. By that time the motor industry 'had come bitterly to feel that no move in monetary policy as recently understood in the United Kingdom, would be complete without special discrimination against consumer durables in general and motor cars in particular'.[6]

Effects on Basic Conditions

On the supply side, stop-go policies did not seem to materially affect business attitudes and confidence during this period of Conservative rule. Suez, it could be argued, was an exceptional event, whilst the period of stop in 1960 was short enough that investment plans by the motor firms were not changed. In 1960 all companies had major expansion plans underway and there is no evidence that any of these were cancelled or curtailed. However, the stop periods did appear to affect trade union attitudes by necessitating lay-offs and redundancies, so inevitably reinforcing insecurity and distrust amongst the workforce.

Regulatory policy and stop-go policies aggravated cyclical trends considerably. They also affected exports. During periods of go there was little pressure on the industry to export. However, one of the intentions of stop policies was to squeeze home sales and so put pressure on the manufacturers to increase exports. Consequently government regulatory policy encouraged a fateful stopgap approach to exports by the UK motor industry. Finally, stop-go policies made it very difficult for the UK motor industry to forecast demand, and so affected the whole context within which management decisions were made. Plants operated for the most part either at under or over capacity, whilst investment planning was rendered extremely hazardous.

Effects on Structure

Regulatory policy had limited effects on industry structure during this period though stop policies did tend to weaken the smaller companies. These not only had smaller financial resources but also, because they exploited fewer economies of scale than the larger companies, provided less value for money in their products. One result of this was that when long waiting lists for the most popular BMC and Ford models developed during go periods, the less patient customers tended to switch to Rootes, Vauxhall and STI cars; but during stop periods, when such buyers could obtain immediate delivery even from BMC and Ford, the smaller companies felt the pinch. Thus the stop periods put some pressure on the smaller companies to merge and effect industry rationalisation. However, stop-go seemed a drastic way to achieve industry rationalisation and was not the government's intention. In any case stop periods didn't last long enough for any of the merger movements it incited to be brought to fruition.

Effects on Conduct

By encouraging exports only during stop periods the government affected firm conduct by discouraging the establishment of an export trade on a long-term basis. Exports were secondary stopgaps to absorb excess production after the profitable home market had been satisfied. For instance, in 1960, when home demand was squeezed, prices in the USA were reduced even though unit costs had increased. Periods of stop also meant a profit squeeze and so discouraged research and development, since in the UK profits were the main source of investment capital for the motor industry.

Effects on Performance

Regulatory policy affected most of the government's overall goals. Productive and allocative efficiency suffered, first, because during periods of stop plants operated well below capacity so raising unit costs and, secondly, because redundancies associated with stop encouraged the trade unions to emphasise job protection at the expense of productivity improvements. Stop policies by squeezing profits retarded industry progress. Stop-go policy also meant that employment in the industry was rendered unstable and beyond the control of management and trade union. Finally, the main intention of regulatory policy was to affect the balance of payments. In the short run stop policies squeezed production into export markets and to this extent was successful. However, in the long run it is questionable whether regulatory policy did help the balance of payments. Stop-go provided little incentive to produce models really appropriate for export markets, since go periods focused the manufacturers' attention on the home market. Furthermore, periods of stop slowed progress in the UK motor industry and so weakened international competitiveness. In the long run stop-go detracted from the overall contribution of the UK motor industry to the balance of payments.

Export Policy

When rearmament ended, the export quotas were abandoned. A clear statement of the government's export policy for the motor industry was made in 1956 when it was declared:

> It is not for the government to export cars; it is for the motor industry to do that. Whilst it may have seen some decline in the share of world markets, it is still the premier exporter in the world.[7]

Though the government disclaimed responsibility for car exports, at the same time it was still 'deeply interested in the export performance of the industry' and claimed it would 'continue to promote exports whenever possible'.[8] In addition,

> All the services of information, help and advice provided by the

Board of Trade and overseas offices for exports generally [were] available to the motor industry; so [were] the facilities for export credit insurance offered by the Export Guarantee Department.[9]

Government policy was to leave exporting to the motor industry. Any government influence on motor exports was indirect through regulatory policy: a regulatory policy which encouraged the motor industry to concentrate on the home market, as from 1953 to 1955, and to turn to export markets only in times of difficulty.

Consequences of Export Policy

The government's lack of emphasis on motor exports had little effect on the basic conditions or structure of the industry but did affect industry conduct, notably designs and overseas sales strategy, which in turn influenced performance.

With few incentives to export the manufacturers were encouraged to focus on the home market and therefore produced designs suitable for that market. As a result the UK failed to produce the economy cars which were very popular in France, Germany and Italy in the sixties and which also proved to have a greater following in North America once compacts were introduced there in 1960. There were at least four reasons why the UK motor industry failed to produce such economy cars in the fifties, two of which were directly related to government policy. First, the government's flat rate licence tax scheme was a disincentive to the production of economy cars. Secondly, the tax on petrol in the UK was lower than that general on the continent, therefore petrol was cheaper. Thirdly, and unrelated to government policy, Britain had a large stock of second-hand cars in comparison to France, Germany and Italy. In those countries pre-war and post-war production had been lower than in Britain and wartime destruction much greater. Consequently in the fifties in Britain there were good substitutes available for economy cars in the form of second-hand cars. Fourthly, the UK manufacturers claimed that when they costed for a hypothetical smaller car they found that they squeezed out value faster than they squeezed out costs.[10] Commenting on the manufacturers' policy of producing models suitable for British conditions, the *Spectator* in 1955 reported that the Swiss called British cars 'old men's cars' because of their antiquated designs.[11]

UK marketing efforts overseas were hopelessly inadequate. A major reason for this was an excess of competition between the UK manufacturers. For instance, in 1957 the UK offered 26 different makes and models for sale in the United States, as compared to six by Germany and five by France.[12] This meant that on average each UK model sold just a few thousand units per year in the whole United States. It would have been most uneconomic to maintain sufficient spare parts to provide adequate service on so few sales; therefore, it must be assumed that the necessary back-up service on sales was not provided. In comparison, Volkswagen sold one single model which underwent no major design change. This enabled all Volkswagen agents to carry sufficient spares without the fear of being left holding out-of-date stocks or new outdated models.

The existence of too many UK manufacturers selling too many models in export markets created a form of prisoner's dilemma for the manufacturers. It would have been more efficient for each manufacturer to have agreed to concentrate on perhaps a single export model. Then the UK manufacturers would not have competed head-on with each other in overseas markets as did in fact occur. However, the UK manufacturers were in competition with each other. Even if they had agreed upon a rational overseas sales policy, the temptation for a manufacturer to break the agreement would have been considerable. Imagine that company A, producer of a complete range but agreeing to export only its small car, saw exports of company B's medium-sized car increase because of a change in tastes. If company A believed its medium-sized car competitive with company B's it could argue that its responsibility to its shareholders made it essential to exploit the market and export its medium-sized car. This would have been so particularly in a recession when responsibility to workers and the desire to avoid redundancies would have provoked such a move. Obviously, in a dynamic context, intra-UK competition overseas was a negative sum game. However, given the UK motor industry's structure of too many firms and a government policy of non-interference, it is difficult to see how the game could have been avoided.

The government's non-interference export policy for the motor industry affected its own overall economic goals for the nation. Economic growth and progress were influenced in two ways. First, the excess of competition by UK manufacturers meant every model achieved low penetration levels in overseas markets, with the consequences noted. Secondly, for the longer run, since no single British model really established itself in any market and as British cars gained a poor reputation for service, the rate of growth in demand for British cars in export markets was slowed. Even where there was excess demand for British cars, for example sports cars in the United States, complaints about unenthusiastic sales efforts were commonplace; and the blame for this

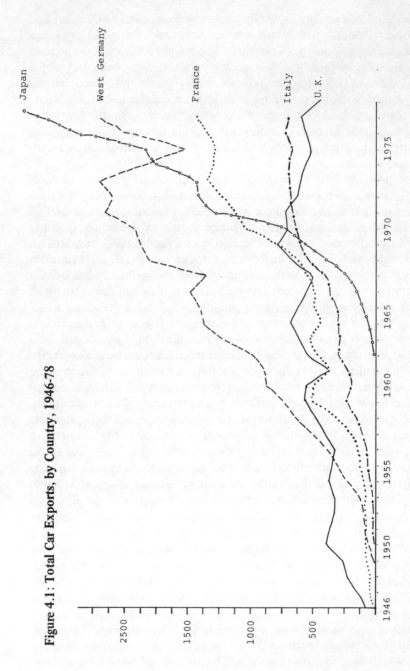

Figure 4.1: Total Car Exports, by Country, 1946-78

Sources: SMMT; Department of Industry.

must be shared between the manufacturers and the government, who encouraged the home market emphasis. Employment instability in the motor industry was exacerbated by the use of stop policies to encourage exports, as noted under our discussion of regulatory policy. Finally, the balance of payments was helped in the short run by stop policies but the failure to establish exports on a rational basis harmed the balance of payments in the long run. Figure 4.1 shows how British car exports showed a dramatic decline in performance relative to the other European producers during these years.

Competitions Policy

During this period, there were two distinct developments in competitions policy. These are discussed under two separate headings, restrictive trade practices policy and mergers policy.

Restrictive Trade Practices Policy

In 1956 the Restrictive Trade Practices Act was passed. Before 1956 the Board of Trade had referred individual cases of restrictive trade practices to the Monopolies Commission. Under the tougher 1956 Act all agreements which fell within the meaning of restrictive trade practices, as defined by the Act, had to be registered. Trade restrictions between two parties had to be registered if they were of the following nature: prices to be charged; terms or conditions on or subject to which goods would be supplied; the areas or places in which goods were to be sold. Whilst some other restrictions also had to be registered, these three applied particularly to the manner in which the motor companies distributed their products domestically. The Restrictive Trade Practices Court did not automatically exclude such restrictions but the presumption was that they were not in the public interest. All agreements involving more than two parties, multilateral agreements, were declared illegal. The main thrust of the Act, therefore, was to force all those registering restrictions to demonstrate that the agreements were in the public interest.

Consequences of RTP Policy. The Restrictive Trade Practices Act mainly affected firm conduct in the motor industry. In the summer of 1956 Austin brought a test case before the courts. Previously the manufacturers had had multilateral agreements between the distributors, dealers and retailers. These the court decided were illegal under the new legislation, though individual bilateral agreements with each distributor, dealer or retailer could be registered. Under the new legislation:

(i)   Bilateral agreements became legally binding and enforceable in
      courts of law.
(ii) Exclusive dealing was made illegal; a manufacturer could no longer
      forbid a dealer or retailer to sell other makes.
(iii) Any person could be put on a list of dealers if they satisfied certain
      conditions.

The car companies were particularly concerned about this last point
because the conditions to be met were undemanding. For instance,
showrooms had only to be 400 square feet, enough to hold two vehicles,
and parts and service requirements were not very rigorous.

Whilst the effect of abandoning the old multilateral agreements had
limited effect on the public, it did remove major abuses which had taken
place within the industry. In 1949 the Lloyd Jacob Committee had
commented,

> We believe, however, that as a matter of principle it is extremely un-
> desirable to encourage any sanction for breach of agreement, which
> is not applied through the due process of law. The complex system
> which is built up by many associations to detect breaches of agree-
> ment may not in itself be positively harmful − although in our
> opinion it is wasteful, unnecessary and undesirable − but the use of
> extra-legal sanctions which may deprive a trader of his livelihood is
> not, in our opinion, justified.[13]

This described exactly what had happened in the British motor industry.
Extra-legal sanctions had been imposed by the British Motor Traders
Association (BMTA) on members who breached agreements and sold
at below agreed prices. The matter came up on the BBC programme
'Any Questions'.[14] Two MPs criticised the BMTA and one of them,
Mr Anthony Greenwood, called the association 'a completely restrictive
monopoly'. Although the BMTA persuaded the BBC to delete part of
the programme it emerged that:

(i)   The BMTA was used by the motor vehicle and the motor accessory
      manufacturers to compel retailers to sell to the public at the price
      the manufacturer had set.
(ii) An offence against any one manufacturer was treated, under the
      multilateral agreement system, as an offence against all manu-
      facturers and was penalised by fines and boycotts.
(iii) 'Investigators', often retired policemen, were used by the BMTA to

find offenders. Although the BMTA instructed these investigators
not to incite offences, it was reported that they did sometimes do
so by, for instance, asking for discounts.

(iv) Private courts, constituted by and answerable only to the BMTA,
were set up to try and punish alleged offenders.

The 1956 Restrictive Trade Practices Act made collective resale price
maintenance illegal. To overcome this the British manufacturers and
foreign concessionaires, in all sixty-five signatories, set up the Motor
Vehicle Distribution Scheme. Basically this scheme to maintain 'orderly
marketing' was a scheme to retain resale price maintenance. The bilateral
franchises which were signed after the 1956 Act all contained a resale
price maintenance clause, although non-franchised dealers were not
bound. Under the Motor Vehicle Distribution Scheme the signatories
agreed to prescribe prices and trade discounts for their products, and to
see that these were adhered to by dealers. The scheme also governed the
sale of vehicles to the trade and to fleet buyers. In 1960 the Restrictive
Trade Practices Court rejected the claim that the scheme, which also set
minimum standards for dealers, gave 'specific and substantial benefits
to the public'.[15]

Although the 1956 Act made collective price maintenance illegal,
individual price maintenance was still acceptable. In the first two years
of the individual agreements the manufacturers took six cases to court
in which retailers were price cutting – two in motor cars, two in tyres
and two in spark plugs. In all six cases the manufacturers won. In all
cases the BMTA provided the evidence and thereby denied their own
thesis, put forward in 1956, that individual price maintenance would be
too slow, cumbersome and expensive to be effective.

For the public it is doubtful whether these legal changes had a major
impact in the market for new cars. Since World War II dealers had been
competitive, in terms of price, through the use of generous trade-in
allowances over and above the resale value of the used car. This form
of avoidance of resale price maintenance therefore continued, though
the new car buyer who did not trade in a car could also now receive a
discount.

The ability of the manufacturers and the BMTA to enforce resale price
maintenance was not severely tested during the boom years between
1957 and 1960. In 1960, as export markets in the United States collapsed
and as the British government began to squeeze the home market,
Vauxhall found stocks of cars building up. For years they had tended
to have the shortest waiting lists so that they were worst hit when the

1960 recession arrived. Their first step was to allow a discount of about seven per cent to dealers, hoping that by offering higher trade-in prices sales could be maintained. When this failed to be sufficiently effective Vauxhall decided to abandon resale price maintenance altogether in June 1960. Prices fell considerably, by up to 15 per cent in some cases, and Vauxhall's sales in July doubled.

The overall impact of the 1956 Restrictive Trade Practices Act, though it considerably involved the motor industry, had limited consequences as regards the government's general economic objectives. By removing the ability of the manufacturers to exercise resale price maintenance through multilateral agreements competition may have increased marginally, though the industry continued to recommend trade-in prices to avoid aggressive competition. A commendable step towards greater equity and justice was made by the removal of the abuses of the BMTA's private courts.

Mergers Policy

Perhaps a fair way to describe mergers policy between 1953 and 1960 would be to say that the Conservative government mildly encouraged mergers. Traditional Conservative *laissez faire* policy meant the government was unlikely to oppose mergers between British companies, and in fact the government also proved unwilling to oppose mergers and take-overs by foreign companies. After 1952, as competition worldwide became more intense, all the pressures for motor industry rationalisation previously restrained by excess demand were set free, and all the smaller British companies sought new partners.

The government's position on foreign investment was clearly stated in 1959. In 1959 Standard-Triumph International (STI) sold its tractor plant to Massey-Ferguson of Canada. Since the sale had general implications for all of British industry, the matter was discussed in the House of Commons.[16] The workers at Standard-Triumph had passed a resolution. In this they stated extreme concern that they should not be bought and sold without consultation. Specifically they expressed anxiety about investment, employment and export policy decisions being made in North America. In the House of Commons the government was questioned about the effect of the takeover on Britain's labour relations and strategic strength and was asked to stop the merger by using the Exchange Control Act. The government refused on the grounds that the merger satisfied the criteria set down to evaluate foreign investment as it affected the national interest. The Economic Secretary to the Treasury, Mr Nigel Birch, stated the criteria to the House.[17] When considering such cases the government examined the impact of foreign investment on likely import trends, export trends and the possible increase in special technology and knowhow that might result. The STI sale was likely to have favourable outcomes on all three. It would also add to Britain's currency reserves and encourage trade liberalisation in general. The government favoured such inward investment which was to the mutual advantage of both parties.

In November 1959 the Ford Motor Company of America bid £129 million for the 45 per cent of Ford of Britain not already owned by Ford of America. This was a considerably bigger foreign takeover than the STI tractor plant sale. Again the Conservative government found the bid to be in the national interest, since it met their criteria for foreign investment. Thus between 1953 and 1960 the government opposed neither national nor international mergers, though it did not actively encourage them.

Effects on Structure. The government's merger policy during this period may have had a minor effect on basic conditions. By permitting foreign takeovers some knowhow may have been imported. Through increased intercourse with North American business some change in business attitudes may have occurred. It is possible that insecurity in the trade union movement was aggravated, as claimed by the unions.

It was on industry structure that government policy towards mergers had most impact. Since the war the government had encouraged co-operation between the firms through various public and private bodies and, as a result, there was open communication between them. Between 1953 and 1960 a number of moves between the firms towards industry rationalisation were made. The problem facing all the UK motor companies during these years, except possibly the two largest, Ford and BMC, was summed up by Graham Turner in *The Leyland Papers*. In a discussion of STI he said,

> For Standard-Triumph, the 1950s had been a period of almost constant turmoil. Its basic problem was lack of size; it was too small to compete against giants like BMC and Ford. It had to struggle to develop new models, and when it did develop them, their sales were seldom sufficient to bring an adequate return.[18]

Amongst the big five Rootes, like STI, was too small. Vauxhall depended upon support from her parent company, General Motors, to survive. The pressure on the smaller companies, Rover, Jaguar, Jowett and Singer, was even more acute.

In 1954 Jowett became insolvent. In 1955 Singer, faced with declining market shares and financial difficulties, was taken over by Rootes. Rover and Jaguar survived by selling up-market, but in what they felt was a precarious position. By 1954 Rover had found the development costs of new models very expensive and therefore risky. For these reasons Rover and STI held full-scale negotiations for a merger in 1954. Poor profits from STI persuaded Rover to opt out.[19] In 1955 a merger between Rootes and STI collapsed because of an inability to agree on the composition of the board of the new company. The fiscal and monetary restraints of 1956 acted as a further incentive to mergers and the talks continued between the firms. All the while there were rumours that Chrysler was attempting to buy out a British company. Therefore, despite a great deal of merger activity and an obvious desire to achieve industry rationalisation within the industry, few changes occurred. In many cases the companies found that the sacrifice of autonomy and the risks involved in a merger meant the final decision to merge was never taken. Only in the case of Singer, which faced bankruptcy, did the merger take place. The theme of a desire to remain independent can also be seen in the STI sale of their tractor plant. For years tractors had been STI's main profit source. The tractors were made under contract from Massey-Harris but it was unlikely that Massey-Harris would renew the STI tractor contract due in 1965. Consequently STI decided to sell the tractor plant before the contract ended. This provided STI with sufficient liquid resources to expand as an independent manufacturer, if necessary, or else to act as an attractive dowry to gain favourable merger conditions. Thus, despite much merger activity between 1953 and 1960, the greatest change in structure was the purchase of the remainder of Ford (UK) by Ford (US). If the government had taken a more active role as matchmaker in fostering industry rationalisation, it is possible that more of the proposed merger ventures would have been brought to fruition. Instead, structural change was limited and the UK motor industry's failure to exploit production economies of scale continued.

Effects on Conduct. Limited structural change in the industry meant the UK manufacturers continued to offer a wide range of models. Rapid growth between 1957 and 1960 encouraged all the manufacturers to produce new designs, since competition in the industry emphasised product differentiation. In 1959, in particular, many technically exciting new models were introduced including the front-wheel drive BMC Mini.

This reflected that research and innovation had not been significantly harmed between 1953 and 1960 by the failure to rationalise industry structure.

The effects of the Ford (US) takeover of Ford (UK) on the conduct of that firm are unclear. In a letter from Ford of America to Ford of Britain it was suggested that the commercial future of the firm would be unaltered. The letter read,

> Our objective is to obtain greater operational flexibility and enable us better to coordinate our European and American manufacturing facilities, and integrate further our product lines and operations on a worldwide basis.
>
> We would like to add that, so far as we are concerned, we intend that your company's operations shall continue under your direction without change in its employment policy or in its development programme.[20]

However, as *The Economist* pointed out, 'one does not bid one hundred and twenty-nine million pounds for administrative tidiness'.[21] Probably the reason for the bid was to be found in two possible developments. First, European cars might have continued to sell well in North America even after the first American compacts were launched there in 1960. If so, Ford (UK) might have needed further expansion to fill North American demand. Secondly, in 1959, Britain appeared likely to join the European Economic Community in the near future. If so, Britain might have become a good springboard into Europe. In a letter to his shareholders, the chairman of British Ford, Sir Patrick Hennessy, remarked,

> other things being equal greater support is likely to be given to the expansion and development of companies in the Ford group which are wholly owned rather than to that of companies in which minority interests are held outside the group.[22]

Neither event in fact occurred: there was no need to produce special models for America or Europe.

Effects on Performance. Failure to rationalise the industry through merger meant that all firms continued to produce at below minimum efficient scales of production, and that too many models in too few numbers were produced by too many firms at too high a price. To the extent that a fragmented industry structure generated inadequate profits to finance future investment in the industry, economic progress was slowed, though there was little evidence of this before 1960. The increased share of the UK motor industry acquired by the North Americans offered scope for additional investment and technology and this may have made some contribution to progress. The increased share of the industry controlled by multinational companies affected employment in the motor industry, since more employment decisions were made in a worldwide, rather than a British, context. Thus labour demand became more vulnerable to external events. However, between 1953 and 1960 no significant consequences for labour can be observed. Finally, in the short run, the increased North American interests had a favourable effect on the capital account in the balance of payments. For the long term, it was possible that increased technology and investment would lead to increased exports. Additional exports might then offset the future outflow of dividends and interest to North American shareholders which the takeovers implied.

Taxation Policy

Between 1953 and 1960 taxation policy acted rather like a postscript to competitions policy. Only one change of importance to the motor industry was made. The impact of this change was felt on industry structure.

In 1959 the government introduced measures which allowed only the first two thousand pounds of expenditures on a car by a company to be deducted for taxation and depreciation purposes. As a result there was a decline in demand for the more expensive luxury cars of the specialist producers. For this reason Armstrong Siddely ceased production in 1960. In the same year the British Small Arms Company sold its expensive luxury car subsidiary, Daimler, to Jaguar. Since Jaguar and Rover produced cars for under two thousand pounds, their demand responded favourably to the taxation change. For Jaguar the taxation change was doubly beneficial. Not only did demand increase but by purchasing Daimler they were able to increase capacity without becoming involved in the government's regional policy.

Regional Policy

By the late fifties the Conservative government had become disappointed by Britain's relatively slow rate of growth. They had also been impressed by the success of planning in France.[23] The government therefore adopted a more interventionist approach to policy.

The first aspect of increased government intervention to affect the motor industry was government regional policy. As part of their local employment policy the government provided incentives to the UK motor industry to locate new investment in areas of high unemployment. This meant a movement by the motor firms away from the traditional areas of the Midlands and South East England. By 1959, all the motor firms had made plans for expansion, encouraged by the rapid increase in demand since 1957. It was the location of this investment the government intended to influence. The incentive to the manufacturers to relocate was government financial assistance and subsidies. The disincentive to prevent expansion in the traditional areas was development certificates. The government controlled the issue of development certificates. The government stopped issuing them for the construction of new plants by the motor firms in the traditional areas.

The government's local employment policy was introduced just before the biggest investment boom in the motor industry's history. The previous investment booms had been in 1954 and 1957. Thirty million pounds and forty million pounds had been spent, respectively. For 1961 and 1962 the industry planned to spend eighty million pounds in each year. The government persuaded the motor firms to spend over half of this in the areas of high unemployment. As a result, there was a considerable impact on the location of the industry which became geographically dispersed.

Effects on Basic Conditions

Expansion meant the creation of tens of thousands of jobs in Wales, Scotland and on Merseyside. As an incentive to the industry to move there, the trade unions agreed to accept lower wage rates in the new areas than in the traditional areas. In the new areas the motor industry agreed to pay the same 'rates and earnings' as those ruling in the district. Initially this meant labour costs would be lower in the new areas if, and it would turn out to be a very big 'if', new workers could adjust to the rigour and monotony of operations in a motor factory.

The relocation of the motor industry also had consequences for the suppliers of raw materials and parts to the motor industry. The motor industry has an important role in the economy in final factor demand. The investment by the motor manufacturers induced further industrial investment by companies which were suppliers to the motor industry. The most important, and the major part of this induced investment, was the decision to build a new steel mill at the Spencer works in Newport, Wales, and to make extensions to the Scottish steel plant at Ravenscraig and the Welsh plant at Port Talbot. This induced investment was estimated to cost £150 million by 1965, nearly as much as the motor industry itself intended to spend on expansion. In addition, Pressed Steel planned to increase its capacity to produce bodies by fifty per cent in order to keep up with forecast motor vehicle production. In accordance with government regional policy Pressed Steel planned to construct a major new plant at Linwood in Scotland as well as factories at Jarrow and Swindon. Bodies for Rootes, BMC and STI would be produced and by 1962 Pressed Steel's total capacity was expected to be three million units per year.

Effects on Structure

The government's regional policy had a considerable impact on the location of the industry. However, the policy did nothing to encourage the further rationalisation of the motor industry which the government had claimed to seek since 1946, and which was essential if worldwide competitiveness was to be maintained.

As a result of the government's financial incentives all the major manufacturers were encouraged to expand to the new areas. Overall BMC planned to spend nearly fifty million pounds to increase capacity to over one million units in 1962. The Board of Trade persuaded BMC to spend over twenty million pounds at places on their list of locations with high unemployment. Completely new factories were built in Scotland, Wales and on Merseyside. All planned increases in BMC's labour force were for the new areas. The government provided 15-year interest-free loans to pay for the new factories whilst BMC financed the equipment. Ford had made plans to invest seventy million pounds when it met with the Board of Trade. As a result of those negotiations Ford agreed to spend thirty million pounds to build 'an integrated car body plant, including stamping, body assembly, paint, trim and final assembly operations to employ about eight thousand in the production of two hundred thousand cars a year' at Halewood, Liverpool.[24] Whilst for Ford this plant was not a first choice location it had certain benefits. First, it was large enough to exploit most technical economies of scale. Secondly, Halewood is not far from a source of sheet steel; in neighbouring Cheshire, J. Summers operated the Shotton Steel Mill. Thirdly, as in the case with BMC, Ford was to get government financial assistance and the trade unions agreed to the payment, initially anyway, of local wage rates. Finally, Halewood is located reasonably close to the major part of the home market, the South East and Midlands. Vauxhall and STI were also induced to expand to Merseyside. Vauxhall built an integrated commercial vehicle plant at Ellesmere Port. They then concentrated all passenger vehicle production at their original Luton plant. STI built a new body plant at Speke, near Liverpool. Rootes was the last company among the big five to announce its expansion plans. By the time they made their decision the government had decided sufficient development had been announced for Merseyside and that further public financial assistance would not provide much more benefit there. Accordingly, Rootes decided to build a new integrated plant at Linwood, near BMC's new Scottish plant. Among the two specialist companies, Jaguar avoided the government's relocation policy by a shrewd takeover of Daimler, whilst Rover decided to build a plant to produce the aluminium-bodied Land Rover at Cardiff in South Wales; ironically this was near the steel mills.

The relocation of the motor industry's expansion plans had negative effects on their costs. This was reflected in that the government's considerable financial incentives were alone inadequate to induce relocation. The government also had to refuse to grant development certificates in the traditional areas. In addition, most of the firms had their original first-choice regional location plans rejected, which implies the industry believed that plants with lower costs could have been situated elsewhere.

Effects on Performance

Regional policy caused little change in firm conduct but had an important effect on overall performance objectives. Clearly the government was prepared to trade off efficiency in the highly competitive international motor industry for lower regional employment rates. No data are available to measure the effects of relocation on costs. However, some comments can be made. Merseyside was not very far from supplies of sheet steel, from the component suppliers in the Midlands, or from the major part of the home market. Therefore, when Vauxhall and Ford built completely integrated plants on Merseyside net cost penalties were probably not very great. The STI move to Speke must have added significantly to their costs. STI's total output even from a single plant was clearly too small to exploit potential economies of scale. Rootes was probably the worst affected. Although the new Linwood plant in Scotland was fully integrated, Rootes, like STI, was too small to fully exploit available economies of scale. Furthermore, the Linwood plant was a considerable distance from the major components suppliers and the bulk of the home market.

Additional misallocation of resources implying higher costs in the industry was generated by the fact that the government only redirected investment. It failed to co-ordinate it. All the new investment which the government channelled to the areas of high unemployment had a significant effect on capacity. In 1960 capacity was a little over two million. In 1962 it was almost three million with nearly one quarter produced on Merseyside and in Scotland. Much of this investment was made by the manufacturers on the assumption that it would help them increase their market shares. Obviously they could not all increase market shares. Government implementation of regional policy encouraged an irrational overexpansion of the motor industry. The extent of this over-expansion is shown in that between 1955 and 1960 home demand had grown at an average rate of seven per cent per annum. If this rate had continued, and if exports had risen by twenty per cent, sales in 1963 would have been one and a half million, or about sixty per cent of capacity. At that time Britain was negotiating to join the European Economic Community (EEC) and the government implicitly suggested that it was here that additional sales would be made, for its own comments on the home market did not suggest much growth was hoped for there. Mr Maudling said, 'No one is expecting to see in the 60s the eleven, twelve or thirteen per cent annual increase in production which we saw in the late 1950s.'[25] Similarly, the President of the Board of Trade told the motor industry to expect a rate of increase in output approximately the same as the rest of manufacturing industry, a single digit growth rate. And whilst Mr Erroll also said that he saw, in regard to the UK motor industry, 'no reason why we should not get an increasing share of the expanding markets of Europe',[26] this viewpoint must have been made on the premise that Britain would join the EEC, for on the 1 January 1961 the first external tariff by the community was to come into effect. As a result Britain would pay 14.8 per cent versus 11.9 per cent for members of the community on imports to Germany; 24.0 per cent versus 16.8 per cent into the Benelux countries; 29.0 per cent versus 21.0 per cent into France and 38.5 per cent versus 31.5 per cent into Italy.

Indeed, the assumption in 1960 that exports would rise appreciably in the future was highly questionable. In Canada new import restrictions had been imposed, whilst in the United States the success of European imports had caused the United States manufacturers to introduce compact models. Both the government and the industry revealed notable optimism, even recklessness, with public money in the efforts made to increase capacity in the industry.

A major consequence of the relocation on performance was the negative effect on the efficient allocation of resources. It also affected employment, equity, progress and the balance of payments. The impact on employment and equity was positive. Over fifty thousand new jobs were created in the motor industry as well as a stimulus given to the local economies. This stimulus helped to reduce the differential in living standards between the areas of high unemployment and the more affluent regions of Britain. The effect on the balance of payments was negative. The implicit increased costs to the industry meant UK cars had to become less competitive in export markets than would otherwise have been the case.

Roads and Transport Policy

In 1953 the Conservative government passed a new Transport Act which revoked the 1947 Act. Most road transport was denationalised and returned to private enterprise so as to reinstitute competition.

After 1953 there was a rapid increase in transport demand both by passengers and for freight. Whilst the number of cars and their usage increased rapidly and freight transport by road expanded, bus and railway usage still remained buoyant. Not until after 1958 did passenger miles travelled by private car exceed those by public transport or freight carried by road exceed that carried by rail. Consequently, in 1955 the government undertook a fifteen-year £1,240 million modernisation scheme for the railways in the belief that the railways had an important role to play in the future and could compete with road transport.[27] By 1959 £587 million had been spent but it had become apparent that even an improved rail system could do little to decrease demand for the private car, even with minimal road expenditures. Whilst in later years more would be spent on the roads and the railways system be reduced, during the 1950s road expenditures suffered in comparison to those on rail transport. In 1956 only £13.1 million was spent on new and major road improvements and even in 1960 only £72.6 million.[28]

Consequences of Transport Policy

Failure by the government to appreciate the nature of the eclipse of rail transport by road transport, and to spend accordingly on the roads, exacerbated road congestion on an already inadequate system. Between 1950 and 1960 the proportion of total consumer expenditures spent on transport rose from 5.7 per cent to 9.4 per cent, of which the proportion spent on road transport rose from 32.3 per cent to 64.1 per cent.[29] For the UK motor industry this neglect of the road system manifested itself in firm conduct. The motor industry, encouraged by government *laissez faire* policy to focus on the home market, designed cars, right up until 1960, suitable for the backward UK road system. This in part explained the relatively poor performance of UK cars in export markets, and the less-than-potential contribution made to the balance of payments by the industry.

Labour Relations Policy

Between 1953 and 1960 the government continued its policy of general non-interference in the industrial democratic process. Still, government policy had a strong influence on motor industry labour relations. First, once excess demand came to an end in 1953, government regulatory stop-go policy began to have a very considerable effect on labour relations. Secondly, the government continued its policy of setting up a court of inquiry whenever the industrial democratic process broke down.

Figure 4.2 shows the inverse relationship between strike activity and production. By using the motor industry as a general economic regulator the government caused considerable fluctuations in production, and so in labour demand, which aggravated labour relations.

Figure 4.2: Production and Strikes in the UK Motor Industry, 1946-64

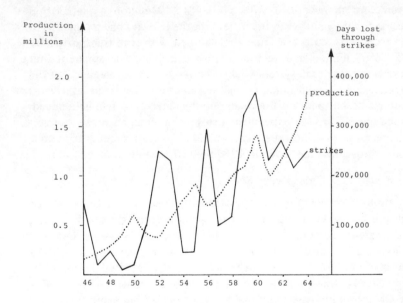

Sources: SMMT; H.A. Turner, G. Clack and G. Roberts, *Labour Relations in the Motor Industry* (Allen and Unwin, London, 1967), p. 110.

The government did not appear very aware that regulatory policy affected labour relations. For instance, in 1956 BMC had to lay off one worker in every eight with no redundancy pay. *The Times* called BMC's action 'unjustified provocation',[30] and in a letter to that paper a Conservative MP, Martin Lindsay, wrote to say BMC's action, 'affronted everyone who has a fundamental belief in the decencies and dignity of man'.[31] *The Economist* reported that Sir Anthony Eden, the Prime Minister, 'nodded vigorously' when Labour members criticised BMC's action.[32] The Conservative government seemed blind to their role in causing BMC's decision, however arrogantly BMC handled the matter.

Only one court of inquiry was set up between 1953 and 1960. The strike involved stemmed from the government's regulatory policy which necessitated redundancies at Ford's Briggs body plant late in 1956. The essence of the strike concerned the role of shop stewards in the plants. At the centre of the 'bellringer' dispute was a Mr McLaughlin, chairman of an 'unofficial' shop committee. When Ford announced redundancies his shop passed a resolution calling for an immediate meeting if anyone in the shop was dismissed or made redundant. In January 1957 two shop stewards in McLaughlin's shop were disciplined for unauthorised absence from work. In direct contradiction of the shop foreman, Mr McLaughlin immediately called for a stoppage of work. For this action Mr McLaughlin was fired and a strike called. At the court of inquiry Mr McLaughlin was found to have been justifiably dismissed. Ford had publicised their intention to discipline breaches of procedure and Mr McLaughlin was not a scapegoat, as the union claimed. The court of inquiry also examined the history of labour relations at Ford. It found that beneath the McLaughlin incident lay matters of a more general nature. First, Ford's procedure to curb unofficial stoppages did not work. Secondly, there was much ill-will between management and labour, and the court found that a section of the shop stewards' organisation was largely responsible for this. Thirdly, the existence of an uncontrolled shop stewards' organisation was undesirable from both the unions' and management's viewpoint.

Analysis of labour relations between 1953 and 1960 finds an industrial relations system that was inappropriate for the UK motor industry. Government wartime legislation was partly responsible for this, for it had encouraged the motor firms to allow many hostile unions into their plants, so creating an all important co-ordinating role for the shop stewards. Government regulatory policy during this period then created additional pressures and insecurity which the industrial relations system could not handle. It was not until excess demand for cars ended in 1953 that the major fluctuations in output and labour demand occurred, the fall in output during the Korean crisis being to some extent offset by military orders.

Consequences of Labour Policy

Government labour relations policy, or lack of it, had its major influence on the basic conditions of supply in the UK motor industry. First, the attitude of confrontation between management and labour created an inflexible, and therefore inefficient workforce. Secondly, poor labour relations retarded technological advance in the motor industry.

Clack has written,

> automation has only been a direct cause of conflict where it has led to redundancy: and redundancy has caused conflict whether or not it has been associated with automation. But although automation has in fact seldom caused unemployment, fear of its labour-saving potential may well have added, during the middle 1950s at any rate, to feelings of insecurity originally derived from the pre-war pattern of large seasonal variations in employment . . . It is therefore not surprising that many were still inclined to subscribe to the view that automation leads to redundancy.[33]

The only strike directly caused by automation in the British plants was that at STI in 1956. In 1956 STI, who had a good record for the motor industry as an employer, planned to retool the tractor plant. To avoid lay-offs they proposed to do this in the summer when motor car demand is usually at a peak and when they would then be able to absorb the unneeded tractor workers into the car plant. Unfortunately that summer the expected peak in demand never materialised because the government introduced a credit squeeze at the same time that overseas sales, as a result of the Suez crisis, declined. STI had no alternative but to lay off 3,500 men as redundant if the company was to survive. STI had already moved to a three-day week and it was felt had only kept the plant running for the benefit of the workers.[34] The two largest unions at STI, the Transport and General Workers Union and the Amalgamated Engineers Union, had accepted that for reasons largely beyond STI's control, namely the government's credit squeeze, not all could work. The Communist-dominated Electricians Trade Union had a Shop Steward's Liaison Committee at STI and they passed a resolution that no labour-saving machines should be allowed to replace labour, and called for a strike. The resolution was along the Communist Party line. The appeal for a strike put the other unions of a more moderate approach in a quandary. They knew that the resolution, in a highly competitive industry, was 'sheer madness' but decided to recognise the strike out of the fear that not doing so in the face of redundancies would drive more workers to the Communists.[35]

As early as the mid-fifties, therefore, the pattern of post-war labour relations problems of the UK motor industry can be discerned. For the industry poor labour relations meant higher costs. Also, since change was opposed, research, innovation and the development of new models was discouraged, so slowing industry progress, reducing international competitiveness and the industry's ability to contribute to the all important balance of payments. Efforts to correct the balance of payments using fiscal and monetary restraint, then created instability of employment in the industry, so worsening labour relations. Thus a vicious circle between motor industry labour relations and balance of payments difficulties can be observed; a vicious circle which government policy was unable to overcome, and which would become worse in the years ahead.

Summary

Under the *laissez faire* policies of a Conservative government the UK motor industry prospered between 1953 and 1960. Production rose from 594,808 cars to 1,352,728 cars, and at the end of the period all firms had expansion plans underway in anticipation of further growth. By 1960 the private car had clearly asserted itself as the dominant form of passenger transport. Nevertheless, overall success was marred by a number of developments. First, the introduction of stop-go regulation of the economy created a situation in the UK motor industry of either underutilisation or overutilisation of capacity, uncertainty for management planning, a disastrous stop-gap approach to exporting and an aggravated labour relations situation. One consequence was slower growth in the UK motor industry than in those of her major international competitors and a declining share of world exports. This trend was not helped by a regional policy which dispersed the industry regionally without rationalising it and so increased costs. Finally, a late realisation by the government that road transport in the future would not complement rail transport but largely supplant it, meant huge expenditures to modernise the railways were carried out, in part at the expense of the road system. In 1960 the road system was not only inadequate and inefficient but still encouraged the design of cars unsuitable for export markets, so harming the balance of payments.

Notes

1. *The Economist*, 29 Dec. 1956, p. 1144.
2. Ibid.
3. See p. 64, where effects on demand are examined.
4. W.H. Nelson, *Small Wonder: The Amazing Story of the Volkswagen* (Little, Brown and Company, Toronto, 1970), p. 225.
5. HCD, 25 Oct. 1960, col. 2125.
6. *The Economist*, 30 Nov. 1957, p. 793.
7. HCD, 8 Mar. 1956, col. 1121.
8. Ibid., 3 Feb. 1956, col. 513.
9. Ibid., 15 Mar. 1956, col. 1945.
10. *Sunday Times*, 29 Oct. 1978.
11. *Spectator*, 21 Oct. 1955, p. 520.
12. HCD, 22 Feb. 1957, col. 726.
13. *New Statesman*, 2 May 1955, p. 164.
14. Ibid.
15. *The Times*, 20 May 1958.
16. HCD, 30 Apr. 1959, col. 1447.
17. Ibid., 2 Feb. 1957, col 574.
18. G. Turner, *The Leyland Papers* (Eyre and Spottiswoode, London, 1971), p. 48.
19. Ibid., p. 44.
20. *The Economist*, 19 Nov. 1960, p. 803.
21. Ibid.
22. Ibid., 19 Dec. 1960, p. 1257.
23. G. Denton, M. Forsythe and M. MacLennan, *Economic Planning and Policies in Britain, France and Germany* (Allen and Unwin, London, 1968), p. 109.
24. Sir Pat Hennessy, *Ford Annual Report*, 1960.
25. HCD, 6 Dec. 1960, col. 1080.
26. Ibid., col. 1200.
27. T.C. Barker and C.I. Savage, *An Economic History of Transport in Britain* (Hutchinson, London, 1975), p. 215.
28. G. William, *Transport and Public Policy* (Allen and Unwin, London, 1964), p. 149.
29. D. Alcroft, *British Transport Since 1914: An Economic History* (David and Charles, Newton Abbott, 1975), p. 115.
30. *The Times*, quoted in *New Statesman*, 28 July 1956, p. 93.
31. Ibid.
32. *The Economist*, 28 July 1956, p. 93.
33. H.A. Turner, G. Clack and G. Roberts, *Labour Relations in the Motor Industry* (Allen and Unwin, London, 1967), p. 93.
34. *The Times*, 4 Oct. 1956.
35. Turner, Clark and Roberts, *Labour Relations*, p. 83.

5 FEELING THE SQUEEZE: STAGNATION, 1960-69

'You've never had it so good', proclaimed the Conservatives in 1959. Macmillan was voted back to office. Yet within the government there was concern that the *laissez faire* policies followed during the fifties were in part the cause of a slower growth rate in Britain than in many other European countries. Accordingly the sixties became a decade of greatly increased government intervention in the economy, first under the Conservatives and then, to a much greater extent, under Labour.

The new attitudes revealed themselves in a variety of policies which had important repercussions on the motor industry. These dealt with the regulation of the economy, international trade, competition and mergers, regional imbalance, labour relations and transport policy.

Regulatory Policy

The establishment of the National Economic Development Council (NEDC) in 1961 represented the first major step by the Conservatives to play a more interventionist role in the economy. Made up of members of the government, industry and the unions, the Chancellor of the Exchequer hoped it would achieve, 'a better coordination of ideas and plans'.[1] In 1963 the NEDC published *Growth of the U.K. Economy to 1966*, a study which attempted to ascertain the effects of a four per cent economic growth rate in the following years.

Late in 1964 a new Labour government came to power. The new government immediately began to draw up a much more ambitious plan than that of the NEDC which it called *The National Plan*.[2] This involved considerably more government involvement in the economy. New government bodies were set up including a Ministry of Technology, a Department of Economic Affairs, a National Board of Prices and Incomes, an Industrial Reorganisation Corporation, Regional Economic Councils and Economic Development Councils. *The National Plan* hoped to overcome the problems of stop-go policies and set a goal of a twenty-five per cent increase in gross national product by 1970.

The basic problem with both the earlier NEDC plan and the later *National Plan* was that neither provided a real solution to the balance of payments problems which had plagued the country since 1945. In July 1966 the government sacrificed the *National Plan*'s growth goals and introduced deflationary measures to deal with the balance of payments.

87

Since the late fifties, at least, Britain had been in a 'fundamental disequilibrium' because of the overvalued pound; a disequilibrium which had to stymie the bold goals of the *National Plan*.[3] For a wretched year and a half the government sought to maintain the parity of the pound to the detriment of other policy goals. When the devaluation decision was finally made late in 1967 it was of the order of 15 per cent. For devaluation to work a considerable transfer of resources to exports to help the balance of payments was required, which took the form of taxation increases, cuts in public expenditures, monetary restraint and wage and price controls. Still, the measures initially taken were inadequate and further restrictive budgets had to be introduced in 1968 and 1969.

Table 5.1: Hire Purchase Restrictions on Motor Cars, 1952-79

Date introduced	Minimum deposit (percentage)	Maximum period for repayment (months)
February 1952	$33\frac{1}{3}$	18
July 1954	–	–
February 1955	15	24
July 1955	$33\frac{1}{3}$	24
February 1956	50	24
December 1956	20	24
May 1957	$33\frac{1}{3}$	24
September 1957	$33\frac{1}{3}$	24
October 1958	–	–
April 1960	20	24
January 1961	20	36
June 1965	25	36
July 1965	25	30
February 1966	25	27
July 1966	40	24
June 1967	30	30
July 1967	25	36
November 1967	$33\frac{1}{3}$	27
November 1968	40	24
July 1971	–	–
December 1973	$33\frac{1}{3}$	24
June 1977	Restrictions abolished on car purchases by companies	

Source: SMMT, *The Motor Industry of Great Britain*.

Table 5.2: Purchase Tax and Value Added Tax on Motor Cars in the UK, 1940-79

Date		Rate (percentage)
October 1940	Changed to	$33\frac{1}{3}$
June 1947	,,	$66\frac{2}{3}$ *
April 1950	,,	$33\frac{1}{3}$
April 1951	,,	$66\frac{2}{3}$
April 1953	,,	50
October 1955	,,	60
April 1959	,,	50
July 1961	,,	55
April 1962	,,	45
November 1962	,,	25
July 1966	,,	$27\frac{1}{2}$
March 1968	,,	$33\frac{1}{3}$
November 1968	,,	$36\frac{2}{3}$
July 1971	,,	30
March 1972	,,	25
April 1973	,,	25**(VAT = 17%)
May 1979	,,	31**(VAT = 22%)

* only on cars costing over £1,000
**V.A.T. introduced @ 10% + car tax

Source: SMMT, *The Motor Industry of Great Britain*, selected years.

For the UK motor industry the government's interventionist spirit of the sixties made things, if anything, more difficult than earlier stop-go *laissez faire*. Government determination to make the plans work encouraged longer periods of go economic policies in the early sixties. When stop policies became necessary, in the later sixties, these too lasted longer. Since the plans introduced no new policy tools, the government continued to use monetary and fiscal policy to control aggregate demand and throughout the sixties the motor industry continued to be very sensitive to these weapons. Tables 5.1 and 5.2 and Figure 5.1 summarise the general trend in hire purchase rates, taxes and production, respectively, over the decade. Basically between 1962 and 1964 the motor industry experienced rapid growth, then, from 1965 to 1969, it showed a gradual decline in production, home registrations and exports. Over the same eight-year period Japanese car production increased tenfold whilst French, German and Italian output all at least doubled (see Figure 5.1).

Figure 5.1: Motor Vehicle Production, by Country, 1945-77

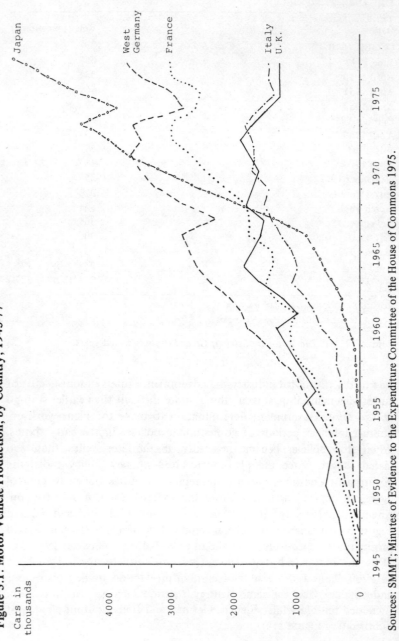

Sources: SMMT; Minutes of Evidence to the Expenditure Committee of the House of Commons 1975.

1961 was the worst year for the UK motor industry since the Suez crisis. At the beginning of the year the industry operated at forty per cent capacity. The government relaxed hire purchase requirements to give the industry some relief. However, in the summer poor balance of payments figures forced the government to introduce a temporary surcharge, to tighten credit restrictions and to introduce a wage freeze. It was very apparent that 'demand for motor cars in Britain [was] cyclical with the rhythm conducted by the government . . .'[4] By the end of 1961 production had fallen to an annual rate of half a million units a year as a result of government restrictions: at the same time, total capacity in the industry was being increased to three million units a year as a result of incentives from the government's local employment policy.

In 1962 a three-year boom in the motor industry began. A revival of export markets, in the wake of improved world economic conditions, and an increase in consumer confidence domestically enabled the motor industry to increase production. As exports increased, the balance of payments improved. The government felt able to remove the purchase tax surcharge and lower purchase tax. Then, in November 1962, the Chancellor of the Exchequer, Mr Maudling, decided to make a dash for growth. He argued that if all restraints on the economy were lifted, an initial worsening of the balance of payments would occur. Later, exports would begin to rise and the balance of payments would move into equilibrium. As part of this plan, purchase tax on cars was cut from 45 per cent to 25 per cent, a rate comparable to other European countries.[5] The relaxation on home sales coincided with a motor boom in Europe and a revival of sales to the United States. By the end of 1963 the industry was working at capacity.

By the late summer of 1964 the balance of payments was in a serious deficit, as Mr Maudling had expected it to be. A general election was called for October. The Opposition Labour Party exploited the monthly deficits to the full. Maudling believed that the deficits were a temporary phenomenon which would be overcome. The Labour victory meant Mr Maudling never had a chance to test his thesis. By the time Labour came to power there was great pressure on Britain's foreign reserves; a pressure increased by Labour's own successful campaigning. Some cuts to the Conservative's growth policy had to be made. Still, the Labour government firmly believed that sustained growth could be achieved, a belief reflected in the *National Plan*. Hence selective controls on the motor industry were avoided for the time being.

From 1964 to 1967 the Labour government tried to resist devaluation. Initially the new Labour government only raised income taxes and

implemented a credit squeeze to control the balance of payments.
Nevertheless, it was enough to weaken the motor boom and usher in
five years of decline. As the balance of payments continued to deterior-
ate, the motor industry was used as a regulator once more. Over the
summer of 1965 car licence fees were increased and credit restrictions
tightened further. Determined not to be a devaluation party the Labour
government introduced additional deflationary measures in 1966. These
included abandonment of the *National Plan*, a price freeze, a change in
investment incentives and more restrictions on the motor industry. The
1966 Motor Show held in October opened to, 'a cacophony of complaints
about governmental unfairness to Britain's biggest export industry'.[6]
Yet, so long as protection of the pound was the government's top
priority, little relief could be expected for the motor industry. Early
in 1967 the Prices and Incomes Board allowed BMC and Ford to raise
prices by between ten and fifteen pounds. The move evoked the
comment that,

> all the motor makers have driven coach and horses through the price
> freeze. The whole range of increases looks very much like part of a
> deal between the government and the motor industry, who [sic] had
> been singled out for punishment last July, but are still far the biggest
> exporters in the country.[7]

By the summer of 1967 the government's prolonged squeeze eventually
had some effect on the value of sterling. In appreciation of the heavy
burden born by the motor industry, the government relaxed credit restrictions on cars. Further relaxation followed later in the summer. Home
sales increased. However, it was an Indian summer for the industry. In
the autumn the balance of payments deteriorated once more and the
government, after three miserable years of resistance, finally had to
devalue in November 1967.

Post-devaluation measures served to reduce estimated annual home
car sales from 1.3 million to 1.1 million.[8] Petrol taxes, car licences and
credit restrictions were increased. The 1968 budget cut aggregate demand
by a further £975 million. Purchase tax was increased and petrol tax
and car licences raised again. Failure to effectively restrain wages meant
real incomes grew, necessitating more restraint later in the year, including
further restrictions on the motor industry. Purchase tax was raised once
more and credit restrictions tightened again. Justifying the new measures
in the House of Commons, the Chancellor used language which would
have been a credit to Lewis Carroll. He said, 'prices are better, at least

lower than expected, and consumption, partly as a result is higher, which in a sense means worse'.[9] Finally, in 1969, the government's policies had their required effect on aggregate demand. Home sales of new cars fell.

Following devaluation car exports increased. In addition export prices could be set at more profitable levels. For instance, BMC reduced prices in Europe by just twelve per cent.[10] This reflected the negligible profits on exports in previous years. Exports to Canada, Australia and West Germany doubled, to the United States they increased fourfold. The government's restraints in 1969 put more pressure on the motor firms and exports increased further. Still, home sales were so low that the motor industry pleaded with the government for some relief. For example, Rootes-Chrysler reported negligible profits despite exporting 56 per cent of production, whilst British Leyland and Ford claimed profits were insufficient to cover planned investment expenditures.[11] In November 1969 the Prime Minister devoted a whole day to a meeting of the NEDC subcommittee on the motor industry, but, despite threats by the industry that investment would be cut, no change in policy materialised even though the motor industry had earned over one billion dollars in exports that year, 16 per cent of all manufactured exports for the year. In the House of Commons the Chancellor of the Exchequer said that high profits had to be earned overseas.[12] By the end of 1969 tough government restrictions meant that the motor industry was operating at about fifty per cent of capacity.

Effects on Basic Conditions

On the supply side, the long periods of stop and go between 1961 and 1969 mainly affected attitudes. The short period of restraint in 1961 did not have major effects on the motor industry's expansion plans. As in 1953 and 1957, recovery came quickly enough to avoid harming business confidence. In comparison the slump from 1965 was sufficiently long to create business pessimism. In 1967 *The Economist* commented,

> a third year of slipping production is about as much as an industry so geared for expansion can take without loss of nerve.[13]

In the second half of the sixties real investment in the industry fell and over £400 million worth of investment planned between 1965 and 1969 was never made.[14] The long years of stop also affected labour relations. These became more troubled and hostile towards the end of the decade. Constant redundancy and short time were a factor in making the workforce more responsive to the demands of militants.

On the demand side government policy had a strong effect. Maudling's dash for growth created a spectacular increase in car demand until 1964. The Labour government's defence of the pound caused home demand to decline until 1969. After 1965 restrictions on home demand caused the manufacturers to make greater efforts to sell overseas and the proportion of production going to overseas markets significantly increased. However, the home market was squeezed so hard that for most firms their break-even point approached or even exceeded expected capacity.[15]

Effects on Structure

The early boom years of the sixties had limited effect on industry structure. The prospect of entry to the EEC and government financial aid were sufficient to make each and every manufacturer carry out large investment plans in the early sixties. Consequently by 1964, although industry capacity had been increased to nearly three million units a year, Britain still had too many producers, and between 1965 and 1969 all companies operated at below capacity. This created pressures for the rationalisation of industry structure which are discussed under mergers policy below.

Failure of the Prices and Incomes Board to control wages affected industry costs, particularly in 1968. At a time of price restraint wage costs to the motor industry increased, so further reducing profits and limiting available investment funds.

Effects on Conduct

Government regulatory policy affected pricing behaviour. Until 1967 an overvalued pound meant that overseas prices had to be kept at levels which made little contribution to profits.[16] After 1966 home prices were also held down by the government's prices and incomes policies. As a result profits were squeezed, and one consequence of low profits was a reduction in research and investment expenditures. Consequently, in the late sixties and early seventies, few new models were produced by the UK motor industry.

Effects on Performance

Government regulatory policy had consequences for productive and allocative efficiency, progress, employment and the balance of payments.

Maudling's boom of the early sixties created an overexpansion of the motor industry without a rationalisation of industry structure. This was particularly harmful for the UK motor industry in that, by 1965, the European motor industry experienced overcapacity, so intensifying international competition. The failure to rationalise meant that between 1965 and 1969 the UK motor industry consisted of manufacturers who were too small and failed to exploit potential economies of scale, and who also operated well below capacity. Unit costs rose at a time when prices were frozen and so profits fell to inadequate levels. The motor industry paid heavily for the government's reluctance to devalue in terms of productive and allocative efficiency.

Progress also suffered. Inadequate profits slowed investment and the research and development necessary for new models and increased productivity. Figures 4.1 and 5.1 show how poorly the British motor industry progressed in comparison to the European and Japanese. Constant restraint harmed employment and employment stability in the second half of the decade. In both the traditional and new motor manufacturing areas of Britain there were frequent lay-offs and short-time workings. Failure of the industry to grow reduced the number of new jobs created and created labour insecurity. In the long run even the balance of payments suffered. Initially an overvalued pound discouraged exports. Although government restraints led to short-run increases in exports, in the long run exports were reduced. Poor profits and a failure to invest and develop new models slowed progress in the industry. As a result, productivity increased more slowly in Britain, and international competitiveness declined. Clearly, an earlier devaluation would have significantly helped the motor industry.

Taxation Policy

Taxation policy during this period is really an addendum to regulatory policy. First, the government raised licence fees and changed purchase tax on several occasions as part of regulatory policy. However, a further significant effect of taxation policy was a new registration system introduced in 1967. In 1967 the system of registration plates was changed. The start of the new model year for cars, on licence plates, was changed from January to August of the previous year. This encouraged additional home sales of cars in the autumn and early winter and discouraged them in the late summer. Consequently, car demand was redistributed from traditionally peak demand periods to a traditional period of low demand. This helped smooth the seasonal cycle of demand in the motor industry. As a result, employment stability was improved.

Export Policy

The precarious state of the balance of payments during the sixties meant that the government was intensely interested in the success of the country's leading exporter. During these years the government ener-getically pursued a number of policies which influenced the motor industry's export performance. First, considerable efforts were made during this period to join the EEC. Secondly, the government negotiated for lower international tariffs as part of the Kennedy Round. Thirdly, the government used fiscal and monetary policy to reduce home demand for cars with the intention of squeezing yet more cars into the export markets.

By the sixties the Conservative government, which had originally rejected the concept of the EEC in the 1950s, had re-evaluated the situation. It now felt Britain should join. However, despite determined efforts by the Conservatives and later by Labour, the French opposed British entry and in both 1962 and 1967 vetoed Britain's application to join. Notwithstanding the disappointment for the motor industry of the vetos on EEC entry, trade conditions were eased during the sixties as part of the Kennedy Round. Tariffs on cars imported to Britain fell from $33\frac{1}{3}$ per cent to 30 per cent in 1962. They were then slowly re-duced to 17 per cent in 1969. As far as the UK motor industry was concerned, however, the government was not sufficiently aggressive in pursuing tariff cuts on cars. For example in 1967, the year of the second veto on EEC entry, the government provided weak opposition to a successful proposal by the French during the Kennedy Round that motor vehicles with engines over 2,800 cubic capacity be excluded from cuts in the EEC external tariff. Although the French were mainly concerned to protect the uncompetitive Berliet truck producer, it also served to protect the French car producers, who manufactured few large-engined cars, from the powerful British Jaguars, Rovers and Humbers. Finally the government continued to use regulatory policy as an incentive to export more cars. These three policies, EEC entry, Kennedy Round cuts and regulatory policy, had a notable impact on basic conditions, conduct and performance.

Consequences of Export Policy

On the supply side of basic conditions, lower tariffs in the sixties en-couraged more international trade in cars and components. For instance, it made the creation of Ford of Europe in 1968 worthwhile; an organisa-tion whose successful co-ordination of Ford of Britain and Ford of Germany, as well as other of Ford's European operations, spearheaded Ford's remarkable success in Europe in the following years. Whilst Ford of Europe was the most notable outcome of tariff reductions, all com-panies increased their foreign components content. Still, the effects of lower tariffs can be overemphasised and in terms of attitude the British manufacturers continued to see the home market as the major market. In 1968 *Business Week* reported the Chief of World Sales for BMC as saying, 'Our export business grew up as a Saturday afternoon exercise done after the week's work for the home market was finished', and went on to suggest that that attitude was still prevalent.[17] On the demand side of basic conditions, as trade barriers were lowered during the 1960s, both overseas demand for British cars and British demand for foreign cars increased. It was not until the 1970s, however, that any drastic change in the pattern of trade occurred and in 1969 imports to Britain still accounted for less than ten per cent of sales, considerably less than imports into the EEC countries.

As tariffs fell during the sixties international competition increased, a trend intensified by overcapacity in the European motor industry and the rapid rise of the Japanese motor industry under the influential encouragement of the Ministry of Industry, Trade and Investment (MITI). In Europe, VW and Auto-Union merged, Fiat and Citroën joined together, and Peugeot and Volvo agreed to co-operate. Fiat built a motor plant in the USSR. Whilst BMC aspired to build a motor plant in Rumania, the contract was given to Renault, because, said BMC, Renault received better government support. In Britain intensified competition stimulated a series of mergers which are discussed below under mergers policy.

In the early 1960s the UK manufacturers were optimistic that Britain would enter the EEC. The UK motor industry enthusiastically supported the removal of trade barriers in order to be able to exploit newly created capacity: British cars were even sold at a loss in the EEC in anticipation of entry and increased sales and market shares there. At that time, British designs were technically highly advanced and VW was said to be greatly impressed with the small BMC front-wheel-drive saloons whose innovative designs it, the Japanese, Italians, French and even Americans successfully emulated and improved more than a decade later. The first Ford Cortina, introduced in 1962, was an acknowledged triumph of product planning. By the late 1960s several years of recession had lowered the morale of management and labour, few new models had been introduced or were planned, and criticism of the quality of British cars was rife. In July 1967 *Which?* magazine reported an average 27 defects on the British cars it tested, and in its April 1969 issue found the quality of a Volvo was superior to all the equivalent British offerings. When the second veto on EEC entry was made in 1967 much of the UK motor industry's optimism and competitive advantage had already been lost.

Performance in the motor industry suffered from export policy, as implemented. Failure to enter the EEC, government regulatory policy and the timing and nature of lower tariffs all had negative effects on allocative efficiency, progress and the balance of payments. Failure to enter the EEC in 1962 contributed to the existence of additional excess capacity in the UK motor industry in the later sixties; excess capacity which UK competitions policy, by failing to achieve industry rationalisation, encouraged in any case. Consequently, unless there was unusual stimulation of income demand, as occurred in 1963, plants operated at below capacity, implying higher unit costs and a misallocation of resources. The way in which regulatory policy was used during the sixties meant progress in the industry was slowed. Whilst exports did increase in the short run in response to restraint at home, as intended, home sales always declined more rapidly. As a result, during the second half of the decade overall demand was squeezed and there was little incentive for the UK motor industry to invest in new plant and models. This was at a time of heavy investment and modernisation by the Japanese and Europeans. The prolonged squeeze harmed British international competitiveness in the long run and hence progress. The lowering of tariffs over the decade accompanied a decline in British international competitiveness. Throughout the decade the British share of most markets outside the European Free Trade Area (EFTA) fell. Britain's share of world car markets, 25 per cent in 1960, was halved. The UK motor industry failed to make the contribution to the balance of payments that had been expected of it at the beginning of the decade during the early optimistic days of economic planning and before the EEC vetos. To some extent, the failure of the home market to grow put pressure on the components industry to export. Between 1965 and 1969 the value of parts and accessories exported from Britain doubled and, by 1979, surpassed the value of finished cars exported.

Competitions Policy

Important developments in three areas of competitions policy occurred during this period. These are examined separately; first, mergers between British companies, secondly, multinational developments and, lastly, changes in the area of restrictive trade practices.

Mergers Policy

The Monopolies and Mergers Bill of 1965 extended the role and increased the size of the Monopolies Commission. Following the Act, the Commission could regulate prices, prohibit acquisitions, impose conditions on acquisitions and dissolve mergers or acquisitions.

The establishment of the Industrial Reorganisation Corporation (IRC) in 1966, however, had greater repercussions for the motor industry. Instead of being passively in favour of mergers in the motor industry, as it had been before, the government, through the IRC, became actively involved in promoting them. During these years the government decided that only one merger in the UK motor industry even needed referring to the Monopolies Commission, and this one the Commission found to be in the public interest.

Consequences of Mergers Policy. With the government's blessing, a number of mergers took place in the 1960s which considerably altered industry structure. The first major one occurred in 1961. Leyland, a lorry and bus producer, made a somewhat bizarre diversification into the motor industry when they purchased STI. As an independent mass producer STI had become too small to survive and the 1960 recession had created great financial difficulty for the company. However, with Leyland's financial resources and an upgrading of the product line to give a more luxurious image, the company flourished during Maudling's dash for growth in 1963 and 1964, by which time the company was well established and profitable.

The 1965 deflation put considerable pressure on all the manufacturers and led to a series of mergers. In an attempt to lower costs through vertical integration, BMC purchased the only remaining large independent body supplier, Pressed Steel. Since Pressed Steel supplied the independent Rover and Jaguar companies with bodies, the merger created a conflict of interests for BMC and so was referred to the Monopolies Commission. The Commission approved the merger on the grounds that it added to efficiency in the industry, though this is debatable.[18] However, dependency upon BMC for bodies, added to increased European competition and the deflation of 1965, made it clearly apparent to the two specialist companies, Rover and Jaguar, that their survival depended upon some form of amalgamation with one of the larger companies. In the summer of 1965 Jaguar agreed to join with BMC to form British Motor Holdings (BMH), though a condition of the merger was that Jaguar would continue to be run autonomously. As a defensive measure against an overly large BMH, Leyland absorbed Rover at the end of 1965. This meant the British-owned sector of the UK motor industry was effectively divided into two companies, Leyland and BMH.

As early as 1965 Leyland and BMH had had discussions without any government prompting.[19] Both sides agreed that some form of amalgamation would be advantageous. As so often had occurred in the motor industry, problems arose over the means by which the union should take place. Ostensibly the timing was unsuitable, so merger plans were shelved. However, by 1967, three years of decline in the UK motor industry meant that both BMH and Leyland were considerably smaller than either Fiat or Volkswagen. As the government saw BMH's market share and profits decline, it became convinced that a merger between BMH and Leyland was essential if the British-owned sector of the UK motor industry was to survive into the seventies. The IRC was used to achieve this goal.

The IRC had been set up in 1966. Losses by BMH the same year and the declining share of the home market going to British-owned companies made the motor industry a prime target for the new body. Early in 1967, the head of the IRC, Sir Frank Kearton, received permission from Leyland and BMH to make a private investigation of the two companies. He did this in the light of a recent Ministry of Technology survey which had concluded, first, that both companies were too small to survive as independents and, secondly, that BMH was not very efficient and needed reorganisation and a new management. At the same time, the managing director of Leyland, Sir Donald Stokes, assessed the impact of the merger. He decided that despite BMH's current losses and disorganisation, a merger would give a fair chance of survival for a British-owned motor manufacturer. By October 1967 the government had become impatient with the lack of progress in the merger talks. Accordingly, the Prime Minister had the heads of the two companies to dinner to add encouragement to their efforts. Still, the companies found it impossible to settle on terms satisfactory to both sides. The talks dragged on. Kearton of the IRC made considerable efforts to keep the two together in discussions. Eventually, in January 1968, with much ill feeling on both sides, an agreement was reached. A major incentive to the merger was a £25 million loan on favourable terms from the IRC. It is impossible to know how much credit for the successful amalgamation must go to the perseverance of the government. Without it, it seems Leyland, less than awed by BMH's management, which clearly disdained formal education and hired a single university graduate in 1967, might have abandoned the merger plans. It is idle to speculate on what might otherwise have occurred, though it has been suggested that Leyland would have been wiser to have waited whilst BMH's financial position deteriorated, as seemed likely, and then bought up the pieces.

The new company was called British Leyland (BL). Upon consideration of its accumulation of many outdated plants, its inadequate, dated and too broad product line, and its poorly co-ordinated, highly dispersed marketing network, one government official concluded that the new managing director, Sir Donald Stokes, formerly of Leyland, was undertaking 'the toughest management job in British industry'.[20] In terms of sales, BL compared satisfactorily with other European giants. In 1968 BL sales were $1.9 billion, Volkswagen's were $2.5 billion and Fiat's were $1.7 billion.[21] However, in terms of model ranges and productivity, the new organisation was weak. It produced twice as many models as General Motors did in the United States, but produced only one-fifth the output.[22] Thus, although BL was the fifth largest motor manufacturer in the world, it still failed to exploit all available economies of scale. This, added to low capital per worker and the poor British labour relations system, meant that 185,000 employees at BL produced $1.9 billion of sales. At Chrysler in the USA, a similar labour force produced $5.65 billion of sales,[23] and by all world standards BL's productivity was low.

In the years following the merger few of these problems were rectified. The model range was not significantly reduced and few new models were developed, though one new ex-BMH model, the Maxi, was introduced after considerable revision to eliminate an unacceptable, boxy appearance. The overall impression of the merger is that just as Morris had appeared to inject Austin with inefficiency after 1952, so did BMH similarly inject Leyland after 1968.

The history of mergers in the British industry suggests that without the government to act as a catalyst, UK motor firms tended to continue as independents for as long as possible. This acted to the ultimate disadvantage of the firms themselves, the industry and the country. Against this background the intervention of the government's IRC was to be welcomed. However, the 1967 Ministry of Technology report identified two problems. First, BMH and Leyland as independents were too small. The merger solved this. Secondly, BMH needed reorganisation. The government persuaded BL to put the former Leyland head, Sir Donald Stokes, in charge of the new company. The job appeared beyond him and later, in 1974, and then Lord Stokes, he was removed by the government. Thus the second problem was never solved. Having achieved the merger the government did little to ensure that it worked. Consequently the anticipated benefits of industry rationalisation on efficiency, progress, employment and the balance of payments did not materialise. BL did not keep up with Volkswagen and Fiat.

As regards the second problem, making the merger work, the Japanese experience provides an interesting contrast. In Japan, the Ministry of International Trade and Industry (MITI) had become concerned by 1961 about excessive competition by too many manufacturers, failure to exploit economies of scale and poor quality in the Japanese motor industry: similar problems to those of the UK five years later. MITI proposed remedies not unlike the British: rationalisation of industry structure and a reduction in the number of models. Despite opposition from some manufacturers in Japan, by the late sixties two motor groups, Nissan and Toyota, were responsible for about two-thirds of production. Japanese success in solving the second problem would appear to lie in the complicated but close social, economic and political relationship between the government, the banks and industry which facilitated the achievement of rationalisation in Japan. By contrast, in Britain, the banks played a minor role in industry finances whilst, if anything, there was hostility between the government bureaucracy and industry.[24] Also, the Japanese mergers took place at a time of rapid industry growth, four-fold between 1961 and 1965, whereas the British occurred at a time of no growth, when labour resistance to change is likely to be greatest.

Multinational Developments

Up until 1964 the Conservative government welcomed foreign invest-ment in the motor industry. The Labour opposition frequently criticised such an open-door policy. In 1964 Mr Harold Wilson, with reference to the motor industry, said,

> Do not the [Conservatives] distinguish between those forms of foreign investment in this country which are and always have been welcomed, which introduce 'know how' which we do not possess, or which lead to the creation of new industries, or new factories and employment for our people on the one hand, and, on the other, those which in-volve a partial or complete takeover of existing British firms which are already well run?[25]

Another Labour spokesman commented on the American Chrysler company that, 'if it had to choose between sacking men in Detroit or men in Coventry or Linwood, it would certainly act to the disadvantage of this country'.[26] After the 1964 Labour victory, therefore, government policy towards foreign investment changed to one of opposition, in theory if not in practice. In practice, increased foreign investment in the UK motor industry was reluctantly permitted to take place. When Rootes got into financial difficulties in 1967 and the options open to the government were to allow further foreign investment, nationalise the firm, or let it go under, the government opted for the first; neither

Leyland nor BMH being prepared to buy up Rootes.

Effects on Basic Conditions. The effects of foreign takeovers in the UK motor industry on basic conditions were fairly limited. Increased American ownership may have spurred the spread of North American business techniques to the UK motor industry in the sixties. Since World War II Ford had been Britain's most successful company in terms of sales growth and profitability. In the late 1960s other UK motor firms sought to emulate the management techniques of Ford, and more specifically of Robert McNamara, leader of the Ford (US) 'whiz-kids', and later President of the World Bank. When Chrysler bought Rootes in 1967 they hired a number of ex-Ford executives to replace Rootes family retainers. Similarly, after the creation of BL many Ford executives were hired by Stokes in a forlorn attempt to improve the quality of management.[27]

Effects on Structure. The entrance of Chrysler into the UK motor industry by the purchase of Rootes was an important development. It meant all three big American motor companies were represented in the UK, but nowhere else outside the USA. Despite Maudling's dash for growth in the early sixties, Rootes had been in constant financial difficulties. When, in 1964, Chrysler bid for one-third of the family-owned company the offer was gladly accepted by both Rootes and the Conservative government, who concluded that the move was in the national interest since it brought in vital US dollars whilst control still rested with the Rootes family. Government restraints from 1965 onwards had a dismal effect on Rootes profitability and in 1967 the Rootes family decided to sell a majority shareholding to Chrysler. Government permission was required for this because in 1964 the vice-president of Chrysler (US) had sent a letter to the British Chancellor of the Exchequer in which he made the following commitment:

> Chrysler undertakes that should circumstances arise in which it wished to take steps to acquire a majority holding of voting shares in Rootes Motors, neither Chrysler nor any of its subsidiaries would take action either directly or indirectly to this end without consulting with the British government nor over their objections.[28]

The Minister of Technology, Mr Anthony Wedgwood Benn, was against further American investment in the UK motor industry. He therefore approached both BMH and Leyland to see if either of them would buy out Chrysler and Rootes so as to keep the company British, and offered them IRC assistance as an incentive. However, after three years of government restraint on home demand neither British company had sufficient funds by 1967 to justify such a venture, given Rootes's weak finances. The Labour government was not prepared to take over Rootes itself. Therefore, reluctantly, they allowed Chrysler to take majority control of Rootes. As a result the three big US companies together controlled over half the UK motor industry in terms of market share and capital invested.

The net effect of increased American ownership of the UK motor industry is unclear. On the one hand, after 1964, the three American companies spent more on investment, relative to their market shares, than the British companies. Chrysler poured hundreds of millions of dollars of investment into Rootes, although by the 1970s Rootes's costs were still above average for Europe.[29] On the other hand, it is highly questionable whether there was room in the UK motor industry for a third US company, even with the most optimistic projections about industry growth, if all were to exploit potential economies of scale. Chrysler bought Rootes as a springboard to Europe for when Britain entered the EEC. The long delay in joining meant that Rootes persistently lost money for Chrysler over the following years.

Effects on Conduct. In the past foreign investment had been justified on the grounds that it had favourable effects on firm conduct by bringing in new technology. It is doubtful whether Chrysler brought much additional knowhow, since they immediately began a recruitment drive in Britain particularly focused on British Ford management. Furthermore, Chrysler appeared to add little to research and development. Only one new British Chrysler was produced, the 1969 Avenger. It was an extremely conventional design incorporating little new technology.

As regards marketing, the large multinational presence meant that exporting decisions for Britain were, on occasion, made in a worldwide context. This was shown most clearly in the early sixties after the US manufacturers introduced compact cars in North America and the US market for British cars collapsed. During the early sixties Vauxhall and Ford of Britain made little effort to sell in the United States. For example, in 1964 Vauxhall sold under one hundred cars there. At the same time, BMC sold over thirty-three thousand units Stateside. *The Times* argued that it was 'necessary to persuade the two American owned companies to institute a sales drive in the United States'.[30]

Similar criticisms, that decisions against British interests occurred, were also made concerning purchasing policy. For instance, the Machine Tools Trade Association accused Ford of Britain of unnecessarily purchasing capital equipment from the United States for non-economic reasons. They said, 'We know that in some instances in the past, Ford in particular has imported dollar machines, whether new or second hand from Detroit, simply because Detroit says so.'[31]

Effects on Performance. The multinational presence in the UK motor industry affected industry performance as regards productive and allocative efficiency and the balance of payments. The existence of three US companies made it difficult for them, particularly for the smaller Vauxhall and Chrysler, to become large enough to exploit economies of scale. At the same time powerful US parents ruled out the likelihood of effecting industry rationalisation through merger. Whilst the considerable inflow of investment funds helped the balance of payments, these benefits were partially offset, as seen, by the nature of the US companies export policies to North America.

Restrictive Trade Practices

Although during the 1960s legislation dealing with restrictive trade practices was changed, the effects on the motor industry were limited. In 1961 car guarantees were changed to comply with the Sale of Goods Act. In 1964 the Resale Price Maintenance Act was repealed. In 1963 and 1966 respectively, the Monopolies Commission investigated firms supplying electrical equipment to the motor industry,[32] and firms supplying wire harnesses to the motor industry.[33] These matters affected firm conduct.

Consequences of Restrictive Trade Practices Policy. Before 1961, when signing new car guarantees, customers also signed away some of their rights under the Sale of Goods Act. For example, they agreed to pay for labour charges on warranty work. In 1961 the British Standards Institute made a strong criticism of this practice raising the possibility of legal action, with the consequence that manufacturers changed their warranties to comply with the Sale of Goods Act.

The repeal of the Resale Price Maintenance Act in 1964 had limited impact on the motor industry, though it was important for the economy as a whole. Since 1959 resale price maintenance had not been strictly adhered to by the UK motor industry. Furthermore, since most new car sales involved a trade-in, inflated trade-in prices had been used to circumvent resale price maintenance.

In both cases investigated by the Monopolies Commission which affected the motor industry no exploitation of the manufacturers was found. All the equipment examined, for instance wire harnesses, was original equipment on a car and usually lasted the car's lifetime. Not surprisingly it was found the manufacturers exercised counter-vailing power over monopolistic suppliers. The most remarkable thing about these reports by the Monopolies Commission was that the Commission had ever undertaken them in the first place, given its small staff.

Regional Policy

In the prosperity of the late fifties all the motor manufacturers had undertaken bold expansion plans to new locations, with governmental blessing and financial aid. This had been done by each manufacturer in the hope of increasing market shares; obviously something not all could do. The increased capacity enabled a rapid increase in production during Maudling's dash for growth from 1962 to 1964, but the government-inspired market contraction of the second half of the decade discouraged much further investment in the new regions. Nevertheless, repercussions of the investments undertaken at the beginning of the decade continued throughout the 1960s.

Consequences of Regional Policy

Regional expansion created labour relations problems. It had been hoped that workers in the new areas would be grateful for the new high-paying jobs and that the factories in the new regions would be less hampered with the problems of piecework. Instead, the new areas became charac-terised by labour militancy and management frustration. The reasons for labour difficulties were partly economic, partly sociological. The people of Merseyside and Scotland had traditionally worked in the ship-yards, down the mines and on the docks. There the work was hard but offered some variety. In comparison, work in the new motor plants was clean, light and high-paying. It was also soul-destroyingly monotonous on the assembly lines. In addition, particularly after growth policies were abandoned in 1964, there were constant lay-offs and short-time operations. During the 1930s unemployment had been very high both on Merseyside and in Scotland, and the instability of work in the motor industry evoked bitter memories of those years. Consequently the frus-tration of the work and the insecurity of employment made the labour force of the new factories susceptible to the demands of militants.

One consequence of the militant demands of the trade unions for parity in the new areas was that the advantages of lower wage costs there were soon eroded, particularly when the costs of stoppages and labour hostility were taken into account. To the extent that regional policy gave encouragement to workforce militancy, costs were increased in the industry and research and innovation discouraged. Increased costs implied higher prices at home and a lowering of competitiveness overseas, thus lowering the industry's allocative efficiency and contribution to the balance of payments. A second consequence of regional policy was a fall in investment. In 1964, aware of the labour problems of the new regions, the small Reliant Motor Company, producer of three-wheeled fibreglass economy cars and of sports cars, abandoned plans for expansion rather than expand to Merseyside when the government denied them a development certificate for the Midlands. Nobody knows what other investment plans may have been quietly shelved by other motor manufacturers reluctant to create additional labour force problems for themselves. Finally, regional policy was originally introduced to improve equity in Britain by bringing economic growth to poor areas. It was clearly not a success in Scotland, either for Scotland or the motor industry. The Scottish motor development consisted mainly of a Pressed Steel body plant and a Rootes integrated car factory, both at Linwood. There, with bodies supplied by Pressed Steel, Rootes built Scotland's own car, the small Hillman Imp. Unfortunately, even in the good years of 1963 and 1964, the car was a failure and sold poorly. It failed for a number of reasons. First, its aluminium rear-engine design was expensive and outdated. Secondly, BMC sold its nearest competitor, the Mini, at a price which did not cover full cost, so poor was their finance organisation. Thirdly, by 1962 there had been a general movement up market away from the very small cars to cars such as the Ford Cortina. As a result many anticipated jobs never materialised whilst the four thousand workers at Linwood soon became familiar with redundancy. What the Linwood experience, which cost the taxpayer about ten million pounds, showed was that regional policy was more complicated than the setting up of new factories and the relocation of plants. The whole Linwood project as a growth centre rested on the success of a single model. This was too narrow a base for regional expansion. It is not the purpose of this book to analyse the success of regional policy. Nevertheless, if Linwood was to have been a growth centre, it would have had a greater chance of success if the government had minimised the risk of failure by attracting other industries in addition to the motor industry to the region. If it had, the failure of the Imp would have been less calamitous for Scotland.

Labour Relations Policy

Government policy towards labour relations in the motor industry
changed radically during the 1960s. From 1945 until 1964 the structure
of labour relations in the motor industry was accepted by the government as reasonably satisfactory. A policy of basic non-interference by
the government in free collective bargaining was the norm; occasionally,
when necessary, courts of inquiry were set up. In the late 1960s the
government attempted to achieve structural change. During the long
years of restraint, from 1965, labour relations generally, and in the
motor industry in particular, deteriorated (see Figure 5.2). The government's response was to influence labour relations with new labour
legislation, the Prices and Incomes Board, courts of inquiry, a series of
government reports and informal discussions at the Prime Ministerial
level.

During any recession strike activity increased. This was the case in
1960. The Minister of Labour was concerned about the number of
strikes and the increase in the number of working days lost that year.
He set up a committee, chaired by himself and made up of leading
representatives of the employers and unions, but excluding shop
stewards, to examine the matter. A statement was published in the
Ministry of Labour Gazette which said the committee had,

> agreed on a number of points on which action should be taken in
> our respective fields to assist individual companies, work people and
> trade unions in their day to day relations . . . We have fully and
> candidly considered the various procedures and we have satisfied
> ourselves that these procedures are generally adequate if operated
> in the right spirit.[34]

Essentially they argued that current methods would work if established
procedures for handling problems were followed: only more consultation, communication and circulation of information were needed.

In 1963 a court of inquiry was set up to examine a long strike which
had occurred at Ford in 1962.[35] The conclusion of Professor Jack's
committee, which made up the court, was that 'following procedure'
at Ford had led to considerable discontent. Implicitly the Jack Report
criticised the strong-stand approach recommended by the government
and followed at Ford. The Jack Report also suggested changes in the
structure of labour relations at Ford. Noting that few of the recommendations of a 1957 court of inquiry had been implemented, the Jack

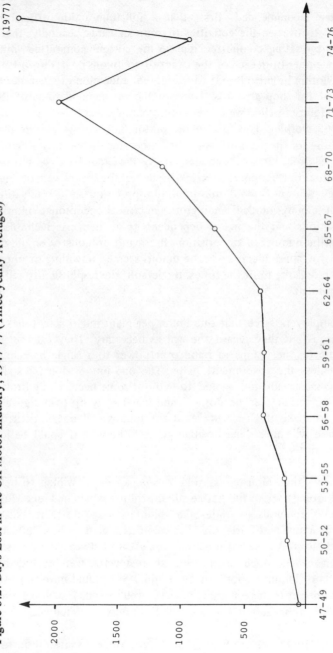

Figure 5.2: Days Lost in the UK Motor Industry, 1947-77 (Three-yearly Averages)

Sources: S. Milligan, *Industrial Relations: Britain's Battle for Reform* (Economist Brief 28, London, 1971); British Labour Statistics Year Book; Central Policy Review Staff, *The Future of the British Car Industry* (HMSO, London, 1975), p. 98.

Committee recommended: first, that a full-time union official be appointed to oversee the activities of shop stewards; secondly, that a six-man negotiating committee replace the current committee which had one member from each of the twenty-two unions on it; thirdly, that secret balloting be introduced; fourthly, that education programmes be established for shop stewards. None of the recommendations of this court of inquiry in 1963 were ever implemented either.

In 1965 working days lost in the motor industry were more than double those for the previous two years. It became increasingly apparent that proper procedures were inadequate, as Professor Jack's committee had reported. Furthermore, after 1965 many of the strikes were of a new sort. They were not about rule book interpretation and demarcation, but about 'bloody-minded' small groups in critical operations exploiting their positions and the many dependent upon them. As technology increased the number of key positions in the motor industry, so did the potential for abuse increase.[36] The unions seemed unwilling or unprepared to reorganise to fit the times. By default, the responsibility fell to the government.

> The employers agree that one union per plant might sometimes be dangerous but they regard the evil as necessary. They can put no pressure on the unions to hand over power to a single bargaining unit unless the government helps. The one union shop is usually anathema, usually not agreed to without some heads being broken ... If something can be done — and it is largely up to the government to make the first move, if the unions will not — then the recession will have done positive good. Otherwise it could be just like old times.[37]

The new Prime Minister, Harold Wilson, appeared willing to help. Perhaps harping back to the Attlee administration which had sucessfully persuaded the unions to undertake voluntary wage restraint, Wilson undertook a policy of friendly discussion as regards motor industry labour relations. A series of meetings was set up between the industry and union leaders. Again, as in 1960, shop stewards were excluded.[38] The courts of inquiry reports in 1957 and 1963 should have provided sufficient insight to suggest that, however well intended, such meetings were unlikely to meet with success. *The Economist* commented,

> it is hard to discuss the futility of the government's latest industrial manoeuvre. Unofficial strikes cannot be abolished by cozy chats at

Number Ten. These are workshop problems that fail to be settled at workshop level, a tiny minority of the disputes that arise every day throughout industry.[39]

The necessity for a labour relations structure to reflect the increased interdependence of one group upon the other as the industry became concentrated was made in two reports by Mr Jack Scamp's Motor Industry Joint Labour Council. Reporting in 1966 on troubles at the Morris bodies factory at Coventry, and at STI, he found that the problems had arisen largely from the piecework system. The system, when it worked, was highly productive but, because of its dependence upon labour peace at all suppliers' factories, it tended to provide highly irregular earnings. Furthermore, when it was working it tended to provide higher earnings for the piecework workers than some more skilled workers received, such as inspectors. Here was another bone of contention. In a year-end report on labour relations in the industry, Scamp found that although there were specific weaknesses in management the major cause of poor labour relations was the total and general incompetence of the trade unions. It was the lack of internal structure of the many unions which made it impossible to enforce collective agreements, and so created a situation of 'anarchy'.

The inefficient labour relations framework continued on to 1968 against the background of the Prices and Incomes Board established in 1966; hardly an institution to improve labour relations. In 1968, the third year of recession in the motor industry, strike activity increased to more than twice the previous year's level. In October the Secretary of State for Employment and Productivity, Mrs Barbara Castle, called the two sides together for a much publicised 'cards on the table' meeting. Again it was the top union officials and the employers who met. Again, as in 1960 and 1965, the shop floor representatives were not present. Reports on the absence of the shop floor representatives from the Minister's talks quoted the case at BMH where Mr Dick Etheridge, shop steward convener for 23,000 men, was not even allowed to receive telephone calls at work. This man was undoubtedly the most important and influential negotiator at BMH. A member of the TUC General Council remarked that: 'Dick is the only man who knows the way from Longbridge canteen to the works manager's office.'[40] Yet he was not invited to Mrs Castle's 'cards on the table' talk, and without him the workers were not fully represented.

Mrs Castle had made up her mind by 1968 that new arrangements in British labour relations were necessary. It was perhaps unfortunate that

by the time her new proposals were made, ill feeling against the government over its attempts to squeeze resources towards the balance of
payments through the Prices and Incomes Board was running high. Still,
the government was determined to introduce labour reform. The proposals put forward by Mrs Castle were in the form of the paper *In Place
of Strife*.[41] The paper recognised that the existing methods of dealing
with industrial disputes were inadequate and that change in the existing
machinery was necessary. It said,

> Little has been done to reform outdated and generally condemned
> procedural arrangements – such as those now existing in the engin-
> eering industry. Too often employees have felt that major decisions
> directly concerning them were being taken at such a high level that
> the decision makers were out of reach and unable to understand the
> human consequences of their actions. Decisions have been taken
> to close down plants without consultation and with inadequate
> forewarning to employees . . . Unions too have often failed to
> involve their members closely enough in their work, or to tackle
> with sufficient urgency the problems of overlapping membership
> and unnecessary rivalry, which always diminish their effectiveness
> and sometimes their reputation. Many employers' relations with
> unions have been greatly complicated by the large number of unions
> that may have members in a single factory.[42]

Among other things, *In Place of Strife* proposed that collective agreements be made binding, that there be compulsory conciliation pauses,
that there be secret ballots over strikes and that unofficial strikers be
fired. This aroused very considerable union hostility. Rather than split
the party the Labour government backed down. By the time the proposals were debated in Parliament secret ballots had been abandoned
and the conciliation pause and system of fines for unofficial strikes
rendered ineffective.

The Prices and Incomes Board also played a role in the government's
labour relations policy. Trade union antagonism to wage restraint was
reflected in increased strike activity over wage demands after 1966. In
1968 the government intervened in strikes in the nationalised railway
and nationalised engineering industries. In both cases, rather than endure
strikes against the government, inflationary settlements were allowed.
In 1969 a huge strike at Ford occurred. Ostensibly the strike was about
wages and important changes in procedure.[43] However, from the beginning there was a general belief that unions, government and management

saw the strike as an attack on the government's prices and incomes policy in the private sector, not about Ford's settlement offer.

Bad feelings between the union officials blew up in the third week of this Ford strike. Mr Mark Young of the electricians union and chairman of the unions' negotiating committee resigned that position in disgust at the more militant attitude of the TGWU and the AUEF. They asked for an increase in the pay offer and a withdrawal of the Ford procedure changes before they would consider an end to the strike. The chairman of Mr Young's electricians' union said,

> We would be fooling our members . . . if we agree this was a viable proposition for a return to work. Even if we could assume that Ford would capitulate, then the government would take up the battle within twenty-four hours. Having beaten Ford into the ground they would then have to beat the government into the ground. So far as some people are concerned that is exactly what they intended in the first place.[44]

But that is what did happen. The powerful militant sector of the trade union movement, particularly, in this instance, the TGWU (the biggest donor of funds to the Labour Party), was able to exert its muscle and achieve its goals. Again, rather than risk a split in the party the Labour government backed down. Barbara Castle agreed to a settlement which provided all the pay that Ford had offered but only token remains of the incentives to steadier production and higher productivity. The deal was given approval by the Secretary of State for Employment and Productivity. This meant it was not necessary to have it ratified by the Prices and Incomes Board. Since the ten per cent wage increase would not have been acceptable to the Prices and Incomes Board the settlement was a good sign to other militant groups in the country that government defences of incomes policy were surmountable.

Consequences of Labour Relations Policy

The major impact of the government's labour relations policy during the sixties was on the basic condition of attitudes. These were affected for the worse. In the early 1960s the government misread the labour relations situation with its recommendation of a strong stand on accepted procedures proposals. Implementation of these proposals caused labour-management hostility. It took the Jack Report to point out fundamental weaknesses in the system.

After 1964 the government became more involved in labour relations

reform. Yet, despite considerable government energy expended in meetings, inquiries, committees and legislative reform, attitudes deteriorated.
Government policy seemed only to aggravate the situation further. First,
the government continued to ignore the important and powerful shop
stewards. In the motor industry they had a minor role in official trade
union structure but a major role in trade union activity through their
control of the shop floor. Secondly, when legislation was introduced to
update labour relations, the Labour government backed down in the
face of union opposition. Thirdly, by allowing many 'exceptional cases',
the goal of the Prices and Incomes Board to reduce inflation equitably
was thwarted. Fourthly, a period of severe restraint, 1965-8, was a bad
time to implement such a policy. Basically the government showed itself
to be faint-hearted over labour relations. It introduced policies which
created hostility with the unions, then lacked the resolve to follow
through with them. Every time such policies were introduced attitudes
deteriorated. Every time the government backed down from the implementation of those policies, it opened itself up to additional militant
trade union blackmail.

Worsened attitudes had further consequences for the UK motor industry. Increased strike activity in the late sixties increased costs. By
then unofficial strikes affected day-to-day operations. Speaking of 1969,
one company chairman said, 'I can count on the fingers of one hand the
number of days during the past twelve months that our factories have
not lacked supplies of at least one part of a car.'[45] If there was not a
strike in a car plant itself, production was likely to be hampered by a
strikebound supplier. Reference has already been made to *Which?* magazine and the woeful consequences of strike activity and labour hostility
on product quality. In addition, design changes and technical modifica-
tions to existing designs were slowed by the failure to deal with the
problem of piecework and the difficulties any change created for this
system in the car factories. Overall, and not surprisingly, increased
labour relations difficulties as the decade progressed affected all performance goals. Resources were wasted and profits lowered. Progress
was retarded. Strikes jeopardised employment for those in related
industries. Exports were lost when strikes held up home deliveries.

Roads and Transport Policy

By 1960 it had become apparent that road transport would be the dominant form of transport in the coming decades. Government realisation
of this was reflected in a number of government-inspired publications.
In 1965 Dr Beeching's report, *The Reshaping of British Railways*, was

published and advised the cutting of 5,000 route miles, the closure of 2,363 stations out of a total 7,000 and huge staff reductions; between 1960 and 1970 rail staff fell from over half a million to 273,000.[46]

Also in 1963, Colin Buchanan reported in *Traffic in Towns* on the likely consequences of increased private cars on urban areas, but argued that severely limiting their use was impractical.[47] A similar conclusion emerged from another report to the government by Sir G. Crowther who observed that 'a car-owning electorate will not stand for severe restrictions'.[48] But as the use of the private car impinged more and more upon the British way of life, many sympathised with E.J. Mishan when in 1967 he wrote, 'the invention of the private automobile is one of the great disasters to have befallen the human race'.[49] In appreciation of the wider impact of the private car on society (the externalities or social cost problem) the Labour government in 1965 combined the Ministeries of Works, Housing and Transport into one Ministry of the Environment. This wider impact of the car was reflected in that in the late 1960s plans for some urban motorways to reduce congestion were cut back following public opposition to their disruptive effect. The 1968 Transport Act wiped out over £1,000 million of railway debt and advocated 'a new relationship between road and rail' in which they 'should no longer be seen as rivals . . . but should complement each other'.[50] The private car and road transport could not and would not totally replace public and rail transport. Nevertheless, by 1970, despite the most congested roads in the world (63.8 vehicles per mile), despite railway modernisation, electrification and, under the 1968 Act, social service grants or subsidies to the railways, and despite considerable public concern, more and more passenger and freight traffic was being carried by the roads (see Figure 5.3). Government realisation of the inevitable was to be seen in tripled road expenditures over the decade (Figure 3.1), and the expansion of motorway mileage from 75 miles in 1960 to 750 miles by 1970. At last, just as her motor industry began to show signs of terminal collapse, Britain had the framework of a modern highway system.[51]

Consequences of Transport Policy

Considerably increased expenditures removed many of the problems of an inadequate road system discussed in earlier chapters. Basic conditions and firm conduct were affected. First, the building of the motorways and improvement of major arteries meant the UK road system became more typical of the modern road systems of other industrial societies. This meant that demand for cars in the UK became more like demand

Figure 5.3: Number of Private Cars Registered in the UK, 1959-76

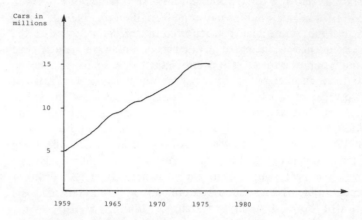

overseas; for example, the Volkswagen only became popular in Britain in the late 1960s. In addition, better roads encouraged more use of the private car and increased overall demand. They also affected firm conduct. To the extent that new designs were introduced in the industry in the latter half of the sixties, these had to be capable of sustained high-speed cruising. Cars such as the larger-engined Ford Cortinas, which became Britain's top-selling model at the end of the decade, typified this development. Finally, increased road expenditures had some influence on performance. By encouraging greater use of the private car a reallocation of resources to this end took place; a mixed blessing which may or may not have been a more efficient allocation of resources depending upon one's viewpoint. Furthermore, by reducing the uniqueness of UK car demand, improved road expenditures created a potential for both increased exports and increased imports of cars as UK cars became more suitable for overseas markets and foreign cars became more suitable for UK roads. However, not until the 1970s did a major change in the pattern of international trade as regards the UK take place.

Environmental Policy

Increasingly in the 1960s, questions about safety and pollution were raised with reference to the car. The United States took the lead in trying to find answers to these matters following the interest raised by the work of author Ralph Nader and Senator Abraham Ribicoff. By comparison, British policy concerning safety and pollution was limited. During the 1960s the British government made it mandatory that the manufacturers fit seat belts to new cars. An overall seventy miles per hour speed limit was imposed in 1965. Annual safety checks on cars were required. Discussions were held with the governments of other countries about standardising safety features on cars. Small government research grants were made for research on safety and pollution. However, British manufacturers were probably more affected by the stiffer United States standards which applied to British car export than by early UK government efforts in this area. The government's low priority for these matters was reflected in the slowness with which changes were introduced. In 1962 the Ministry of Transport announced its intention of making seat belts standard equipment. The policy was carried out in 1967. In 1960 the Ministry of Transport first introduced vehicle tests. Not until 1969 did all cars have to take the test.

Consequences of Environmental Policy

Environmental policies had some effect on car demand. Vehicle tests influenced product life. In 1959 the scrap rate for cars was 4.8 per cent. In 1961 it rose to seven per cent. As the 1960s progressed it approached ten per cent, the same rate as in the United States. The manufacturers welcomed the vehicle tests which by decreasing the supply of second-hand cars increased demand for new cars. They did not welcome the introduction of overall speed limits. These, they claimed, discouraged demand for high-speed sophisticated cars. Certainly BL was criticised on many occasions for inadequate investment in the production of expensive luxury cars such as the Jaguar and Rover whilst in Germany, where no speed limits existed, the sales of BMW and Mercedes-Benz outpaced all other sectors of the car market. Overall speed limits tended to encourage research and development in the areas of safety and anti-pollution at the expense of improvements in the areas of performance, handling and comfort. The final consequences for performance were limited. There was some reinterpretation of progress and a reallocation of resources towards safety and anti-pollution occurred. To the extent that Britain failed to exploit its full potential in the fast-growing sector of high-speed luxury cars in international trade, the balance of payments suffered.

Summary

The sixties were a disastrous ten years for the UK motor industry. Since 1945 the government, largely unintentionally, had carried on a form of guerrilla warfare against the UK motor industry's international competitiveness with its export policies, regulatory policies, regional policies, transport policies and failure to put labour relations on a satisfactory basis. The defence of the pound, begun in 1965 and lasting until 1969, acted as a direct frontal attack by squeezing profits to such an extent that investment and the development of new models were seriously curtailed. The UK share of production by major car-producing countries fell from 11.4 per cent in 1960 to 8.5 per cent in 1970 and its share of exports from 25 per cent to 14 per cent. In the uncertain stagnant conditions of the second half of the decade government efforts to rationalise the industry and improve labour relations failed. And ironically, whilst this giant industry began to stumble, vast expenditures were finally made to provide Britain with a modern highway system.

Notes

1. HCD, 26 July 1961, cols. 220-1.

2. Parliament (Commons), *The National Plan*, Command 2764, 1965.

3. O.E. Williamson, 'Towards a National Exchange Policy: Some Reflections on British Experience', *Bulletin of the Reserve Bank of St. Louis* (Apr. 1969).

4. *The Economist*, 26 Aug. 1961, p. 811.

5. At that time, the sales tax on cars in France was 28 per cent; in Germany, 15 per cent; and in Italy, 11 per cent.

6. *The Economist*, 22 Oct. 1966, p. 187.

7. Ibid., 4 Mar. 1967, p. 847.

8. *The Times*, 4 Dec. 1967.

9. HCD, 16 Nov. 1968, col. 1796.

10. Reports in *The Economist*, 16 Dec. 1967, suggested that BMC believed the elasticity of demand for their cars in Europe was of the order of five, whereas Ford, more cautiously, thought it was about two.

11. *The Economist*, 12 July 1969, p. 69.

12. HCD, 16 Nov. 1968, col. 1798.

13. *The Economist*, 31 Dec. 1966, p. 1414.

14. Parliament (Commons), *Fourteenth Report of the Expenditure Committee, 1974-75: The Motor Vehicle Industry* (HMSO, London, 1975), p. 377.

15. Ibid., p. 436.

16. This was reflected in that after devaluation prices were not raised by the full amount of devaluation, for example, in the competitive European market, BMC reduced prices by 12 per cent.

17. *Business Week*, 27 Jan. 1968, p. 144.

18. Given Pressed Steel's total capacity of over one million units per annum, it might have been more efficient to have had more integration at the assembly level before BMH undertook such massive, hard to digest, vertical integration. The general argument against the 1967 BMH-Pressed Steel merger is to be found in S.E. Boyle, 'A Blueprint for Competition: Restructuring the Motor Vehicle Industry', *Journal of Industrial Economics* (Oct. 1975), pp. 21-41.

19. G. Turner, *The Leyland Papers* (Eyre and Spottiswoode, London, 1971), p. 101.

20. *Business Week*, 21 July 1969, p. 92.

21. Ibid., 27 Jan. 1968, p. 144.

22. Ibid.

23. Ibid.

24. W.C. Duncan, *US-Japan Auto Diplomacy: A Study in Economic Confrontation* (Ballinger, Cambridge, Mass., 1973), pp. 83-100.

25. HCD, 8 June 1964, col. 884.

26. Ibid.

27. A full discussion of this is to be found in A.E. Salmon, 'Inside British Leyland', *Management Today*, 114 (Nov. 1975), pp. 59-61.

28. *The Economist*, 1 Aug. 1964, p. 87.

29. Central Policy Review Staff, *The Future of the British Car Industry* (HMSO, London, 1975), p. 64.

30. *The Times*, 31 Aug. 1965.

31. *Financial Times*, 13 Aug. 1965.

32. Monopolies Commission, *Report on Equipment for the Motor Industry* (HMSO, London, 1963).

33. Monopolies Commission, *Report on Wire Harnesses for the Motor Industry* (HMSO, London, 1966).

34. *Labour Gazette*, May 1961.

35. Dismissals and trade union rights were the main reasons for stoppage at Ford between 1959 and 1962. 1962 was no different. It began in January when there was a sizeable strike over a speed-up in the line at the foundry. A second major strike occurred in the repair garage in August. Management claimed that because of a quality drive and tighter inspection standards there would be fewer repairs and therefore less labour needed in the repair shop. The stewards argued that this would increase the workload in the garage. According to a customary agreement the status quo should have been maintained pending negotiations. However, the official agreement gave management the right to transfer labour as it deemed fit, and Ford, following the recommendation of the government-inspired joint talks, decided to exert that right and refused to negotiate. It appeared that outside the garage sympathy for the strike was limited and when Ford threatened dismissals the strike broke. Then in October a third major strike occurred. A shop steward, Bill Francis of the AEU, called a lunchtime meeting without the required management permission. Following the strong-stand line of the previous year's joint talks Ford decided to dismiss Francis. The dismissal provoked considerable sympathy among the workers because a new disputes procedure had already been approved which would have prevented the need for dismissal. Ford's action appeared high-handed, protest stoppages occurred, and before the day's end assembly operations had come to a stop.

The 1963 court of inquiry was set up in February because of the threat of an official stoppage. Following the unofficial strike emanating from the Francis incident Ford had decided not to re-employ some of the strikers. Some redundancies were necessary in any case and Ford decided to use the unofficial stoppage to get rid of troublemakers. The union saw this as a vital question of victimisation, a matter of principle, and decided upon official action.

The conclusion of Professor Jack's committee was that the company could discharge labour but that it had to be 'fair'. It suggested that those made redundant should have their cases re-examined. Implicitly it criticised the strong-stand approach, given that Ford had overlooked similar breaches of the rules for some time. In the circumstances Ford's action had been excessive.

36. In 1966 a Motor Industry Joint Labour Council chaired by Mr Jack Scamp investigated a number of labour disputes. His reports blamed the piecework structure and the reliance of the industry on shop stewards to estimate the vast number of calculations necessary. The reports found the trade unions to be totally incompetent. The Council noted the remarkable day at Morris when most of the workers walked out in protest of the frequent stoppages caused by strikes by the internal

workers. (*The Economist*, 28 May 1966, p. 996; 24 Dec. 1966, p. 1343.)

37. *New Statesman*, 3 Sept. 1965, p. 368.

38. The extent to which shop stewards attracted the loyalty of workers at the shop floor level was reflected in an event at Rootes in December 1964. The plant affected was the Linwood plant in Scotland; a part of the early sixties expansion already criticised as unnecessary in this study. At Linwood the end of the 1964 boom meant short time since it had at no time operated even close to capacity. By December, all workers had been on a four-day week for five months and the management decided that redundancies were necessary. At this point the shop stewards came up with an ingenious scheme which was adopted by the management.

The scheme allowed two-thirds of the workforce to go back to a five-day week but necessitated that the other third be laid off for one week in every five. During that fifth week financial loss would be mitigated by government unemployment benefits. Apart from revealing a possible management talent among the shop stewards it also revealed a very great trust, among the one-third prepared to face the regular lay-offs, of their shop stewards. (*New Statesman*, 4 Dec. 1964, p. 873.)

39. *The Economist*, 3 Sept. 1965, p. 368.

40. Ibid., 28 Sept. 1963, p. 71.

41. Parliament (Commons), *In Place of Strife*, Command 3888, 1969.

42. Ibid., section 16, p. 9.

43. The strike began in February when the shop stewards' conveners from all twenty-three Ford plants voted to reject an officially agreed pay package deal. At Halewood there was a strike vote in support of the conveners' position, although Ford management made it clear that they were determined not to improve their offer. The management refused to discuss things with the Halewood stewards because their actions were unofficial and therefore outside proper procedure.

By March, twenty-seven thousand were on strike and the cost to Ford was around two million pounds each day, and to the country one million pounds daily on the balance of payments. At issue was a part of the pay package which invoked what were stupidly called 'penalties'. Ford agreed to a substantial pay increase and wage guarantee if part of the pay increase came in the form of an accumulating bonus in return for freedom from unofficial strikes. If an unofficial strike took place there were money penalties to be paid out of the bonus. It was this incentive to increased productivity which justified the wage increase but which annoyed the unions. (*The Times*, 20 Feb. 1969; 6 Mar. 1969.)

44. *The Economist*, 15 Mar. 1969, p. 25.

45. *The Economist*, 'Survey of the Motor Industry', 17 Oct. 1970.

46. R. Beeching, *The Reshaping of British Railways* (British Railways Board, London, 1963).

47. C. Buchanan, *Traffic in Towns: A Study of the Long Term Problems of Traffic in Urban Areas* (HMSO, London, 1963).

48. Sir G. Crowther, quoted in W. Plowden, *The Motor Car and Politics, 1896-1970* (The Bodley Head, London, 1971), p. 354.

49. E.J. Mishan, *The Costs of Economic Growth* (Praeger, New York, 1967), p. 202.

50. P.J. Bagwell, *The Transport Revolution* (Batsford, London, 1974), p. 351.

51. The plans for such a highway system had first been drawn up before World War II.

SUCCUMBING TO PRESSURE: DECLINE, 1970-75

Previous chapters have shown how for twenty-five years, since the end of World War II, the government was able to use the UK motor industry as a policy instrument to help achieve a number of overall economic goals: increased exports in the 1940s to help the balance of payments; regional relocation in the late 1950s to help areas of high unemployment; restrictions on income demand in the 1960s to help postpone devaluation. But in the 1970s the tables turned. Government policy as regards the motor industry had to be sharply modified as the government did what it could to help the much weakened UK motor industry fight off intense international competition. To paraphrase J.F. Kennedy, it was no longer a matter of what the UK motor industry could do for the government and the country, but a matter of what the government and the country could do to make the motor industry viable. This turning of the tables can be seen in regulatory policy, import and export policy, competitions policy, industrial policy and labour relations policy.

Regulatory Policy

Since 1965 the UK motor industry had borne the brunt of a succession of credit squeezes and policies to support the pound. Finally, late in 1969, some improvement in the balance of payments occurred. Despite a rising inflation rate the Conservative government, elected in May 1970, introduced expansionary policies. From 1970 to 1973 the government followed a 'dash for growth' policy and continued with growth policies though inflation worsened and the balance of payments deteriorated. Expansionary measures of 1970 were followed in 1971 and 1972 by further tax cuts of over one thousand million pounds in each year. At the end of 1971 all credit restrictions were removed. In 1971, in cooperation with the Confederation of British Industries, a programme of voluntary price restraint was introduced in an attempt to control inflation. In 1972 the voluntary programme was replaced by a statutory prices and incomes policy and a Prices Commission and Pay Board established to enforce controls. By 1973 rapid monetary growth had fueled the economy to a six per cent annual growth rate.

The increase in oil prices by the Organisation of Petroleum Exporting Countries (OPEC) in 1973 caused a recession of the Western economy which had a disastrous effect on Britain's inflation rate and balance of payments. Late in 1973 the government made some expenditure cuts and, against the advice of its own *Growth Report*, reinstituted hire purchase controls. Throughout 1974 and 1975 the Labour government, elected in April 1974, sought to control aggregate demand in an attempt to defend sterling and fight inflation. Nevertheless, earlier rapid growth of the money supply meant inflation approached a thirty per cent annual rate in 1975. The major features of the Labour government's restraint programme were a 'social contract', a voluntary incomes policy, and traditional fiscal and monetary measures.

Table 6.1: Incomes Policies in the UK, 1945-79

1948	–	April 1950	Wage Freeze	Labour[3]
July 1961	–	Mar. 1962	Pay Pause	Conservative[2]
Mar. 1962	–	Nov. 1964	Guiding Light	Conservative[1]
Dec. 1964	–	July 1966	Statement of Intent	Labour[1]
July 1966	–	Dec. 1966	Incomes Freeze[3]	Labour[3]
Jan. 1967	–	June 1967	Income Restraint	Labour[3]
June 1967	–	July 1968	3½% plus productivity	Labour[3]
Nov. 1972	–	June 1973	Incomes Freeze	Conservative[3]
Feb. 1973	–	Oct. 1973	1 plus 4%	Conservative[3]
Oct. 1973	–	Feb. 1974	7% plus Thresholds	Conservative[3]
Aug. 1975	–	July 1976	6 per week maximum	Labour[3]
Aug. 1976	–	July 1977	4 per week maximum	Labour[3]
Aug. 1977	–	July 1978	10% maximum	Labour[3]
Aug. 1978	–	May 1979	5% maximum	Labour[3]

Notes: (1) voluntary
(2) mandatory in public sector only
(3) mandatory in public and private sector

Effects on Basic Conditions

The context within which government regulatory policy affected home market demand for cars was completely altered in the early 1970s. Since 1945 the UK motor industry had been a powerful tool with which to regulate aggregate demand: a vital precondition for this was a largely captive home market in which most consumers expressed a preference for British makes and retailers, and were prepared to wait for British cars if, in the short run, excess demand was created. By 1970 lower tariffs and faster productivity growth in Europe and Japan meant increased competitiveness from imported cars whose designs, now that Britain had a reasonably modern road system, were also more appropriate. The change in the critical relationship between home market demand and government regulatory policy was forcibly demonstrated in July 1971. In order to stimulate the economy the government introduced measures which included easier credit and purchase tax cuts on cars, and so increased car demand by 43 per cent.[1] Usually the summer is the period of peak demand for the UK motor industry in any case, so that the industry was incapable, as well as unready, to meet the unexpected increase in home demand inspired by the government. In earlier years, such as 1959, waiting lists would have developed for British cars and most consumers would have been prepared to wait. But by the 1970s many consumers no longer felt British cars were worth waiting for. Imported cars were sucked in to fill the gap despite the redirection of 120,000 cars originally destined for export markets to the home market.[2] The government's expansionary policy of 1971 unintentionally acted as a catalyst to a change in tastes for cars in the UK market. The apparent loyalty, or possibly habit, of many Britons for British cars, which had been a feature of the market since before World War II, was permanently weakened. In the early 1970s it became most acceptable to drive a foreign car and the word got around that they, their service back-up, their resale values and their suitability for British roads, were good, sometimes very good. As a result, when deflationary measures, including hire purchase restrictions on cars, were introduced for 1974, the import penetration of the UK market continued at high levels, and the UK motor industry found it had permanently lost its large captive home market.

On the supply side, the oil embargo imposed early in 1974 badly crippled the British economy. Having borrowed from future growth under Heath's 'dash for growth' policy of the previous years, British industry suffered considerably from the energy crisis. For the first two months of 1974, following a major strike by the coalminers, the government implemented a three-day working week to save energy. This caused steel shortages for the UK motor industry which necessitated further reductions in production. For instance, BL claimed they lost production worth three million pounds a day.[3]

Effects on Structure

The government's expansionary policies of 1971 and 1972 caused a sudden and dramatic increase in import penetration into the British market and meant that several foreign manufacturers became significant in the home market. Important barriers to entry were removed as tariffs fell and comprehensive and satisfactory sales and service networks for imported cars were established. Probably, however, the events of 1971

and 1972 only brought forward changes in the structure of the UK
motor industry that would have taken place during the first half of the
decade in any case, as the United Kingdom joined the European Common
Market and tariff barriers fell generally. For this reason changes in
industry structure in the early 1970s are analysed under the section
below on import and export policy.

Failure to control inflation, added to the problems of the energy
crisis, meant that costs rose rapidly in the UK motor industry. This was
particularly so betewen 1973 and 1975, a time when real disposable
income was decreasing and there was much excess capacity in the industry. For instance, between 1973 and 1975 Ford claimed costs rose
66 per cent.

Effects on Conduct

It is very difficult to evaluate the impact of the voluntary and statutory
prices and incomes policies on prices in the UK motor industry. They
certainly affected the timing of price increases. For example, in the
autumn of 1972 BL, who had not agreed to participate in the government's voluntary price controls organised by the CBI, raised prices. The
three American companies, who had agreed to co-operate, waited until
the end of the year, when the agreement lapsed, to raise prices. On the
other hand, all the UK car manufacturers raised prices in anticipation of
statutory controls for 1973. At that time the prices of British cars in the
home market were some 20 per cent cheaper than those of equivalent
imports. By the end of 1974 this price advantage had been eroded,[4]
statutory price controls having lapsed when the Conservative government
left office earlier in the year. To what extent the rapid rise in relative
prices resulted from a catch-up on earlier cost increases, a higher current
rate of inflation in Britain than in other countries, or the time-lags in
international currencies adjustments is impossible to assess. However, as
the relative prices of UK produced cars rose after 1973 import penetration increased yet further.

The long years of restraint in the middle and late 1960s had not only
reduced profits but had apparently also sapped business confidence.
This was reflected in low levels of investment (planned investment was
cut by nearly £500 million between 1965 and 1969), cutbacks in research and development and the introduction of few new models. In
1975 the Central Policy Review Staff observed that many British designs
dated back to the early 1960s and were some ten years older than their
competitors.[5] Inadequate profits in the early 1970s made it impossible
for any of the UK manufacturers, with the possible exception of Ford,

to cover required investment to remain internationally competitive from internal sources. Between 1970 and 1972 total after-tax profits for the whole UK motor industry amounted to less than fifty million pounds, or about the equivalent of the cost of developing one new model at that time.[6]

Table 6.2: Return on Capital Employed for Selected European Vehicle Manufacturing Countries, 1967-71

Country	Percentage
W. Germany	12.4
France	6.8
Italy	4.8
UK	3.5

Source: National Economic Development Office, *Industrial Review to 1977, Motors*, p. 15.

Effects on Performance

In the 1970s a crisis in the UK motor industry, long in the making, finally occurred. In 1975 the director of the SMMT commented, 'In all other countries of the world, without exception, their governments take a positive attitude towards their own domestic industry . . . this is one factor we have been lacking in this country for many years.'[7] To some extent the government acknowledged this. In a White Paper, *The Regeneration of British Industry*,[8] which presaged the 1975 Industry Act, the government noted, 'But the attitude of governments to industry . . . has been too remote, too much coloured by the concept that the government's main function towards industry is that of regulation to prevent the activities of industry, or the abuse of its powers, damaging the interest of other sectors of the economy.'[9] For the UK motor industry this realisation came too late. The long-run effect of years of many regulatory policy changes on the UK motor industry described in earlier chapters (by comparison from 1960 to 1975 there were just three changes in West Germany) had become clearly apparent. Allocative efficiency, progress and the balance of payments had all suffered in the long run. Table 6.3 presents the dismal consequences for profits and investment in the industry. The National Economic Development Council reported that between 1967 and 1971 the return on capital in the UK motor industry was 33 per cent of that of the West German motor industry.[10] Despite considerably lower wages and a devalued pound in the early 1970s, the UK motor industry experienced lower

Table 6.3: Investment and Cash Flow in the British Motor Industry, 1960-73 (in millions of pounds)

Year	Net Earnings	+	Depreciation	=	Cash Flow	Gross Fixed Investment
1960	52.7		31.9		84.6	60.1
1961	28.5		32.6		61.1	88.2
1962	22.3		42.0		64.3	87.5
1963	46.3		47.3		93.6	86.5
1964	53.6		53.8		107.4	89.0
1965	57.2		61.4		118.6	97.2
1966	30.9		66.2		97.1	97.5
1967	(2.0)		69.8		67.8	86.9
1968	56.8		88.8		145.6	58.8
1969	40.0		85.2		125.2	101.8
1970	(2.1)		88.5		86.4	140.0
1971	4.1		102.5		106.6	107.3
1972	47.8		101.1		148.9	81.5
1973	63.3		100.3		163.6	141.7

Source: Parliament (Commons), *Fourteenth Report of the Expenditure Committee, 1974-75: The Motor Vehicle Industry* (HMSO, London, 1975), p. 407.

export levels than France and West Germany and lower production levels (see Figures 4.1 and 5.1). In addition, productivity compared poorly; British workers worked less efficiently with less capital per man (see Table 6.4). Overall, by 1975, the UK motor industry had for the most part become unprofitable, outdated and uncompetitive, so that its ability to contribute to economic growth and the balance of payments was seriously diminished.

Table 6.4: Fixed Assets per Man, by Company, 1974

Ford (US)	£5,602
Volvo	4,662
GM (US)	4,346
Volkswagen	3,632
Opel	3,612
Ford (Germany)	3,608
Fiat	3,160
Saab	3,141
Daimler-Benz	2,694
Ford (UK)	2,657
Renault	2,396
Chrysler (UK)	1,456
Vauxhall	1,356
BL	920

Source: Parliament (Commons), *Fourteenth Report of the Expenditure Committee, 1974-75: The Motor Vehicle Industry* (HMSO, London, 1975), p. 36.

It is difficult to be precise in pinpointing the time when the UK motor industry went from boon to boon-doggle, when it ceased to be a leading sector and became a lame duck. According to one indicator the turning point was 1970. Some stock market analysts claim the stock market is a good predictor of events. In 1970 BL shares began to decline seriously in value. This reflected investor doubts about the ability of the only remaining large British car manufacturer to survive. In a world of increasingly intense competition, in addition to rapid Japanese growth in vehicle production, Spain, Korea, Mexico, Brazil and the Eastern European countries all planned expansion of their motor industries in the 1970s, the onslaught of government policy and the UK labour relations system over the long run had proved, to the stock market, too much for mediocre management.[11]

Figure 6.1: New Car Registrations in the UK and Imports, 1945-77

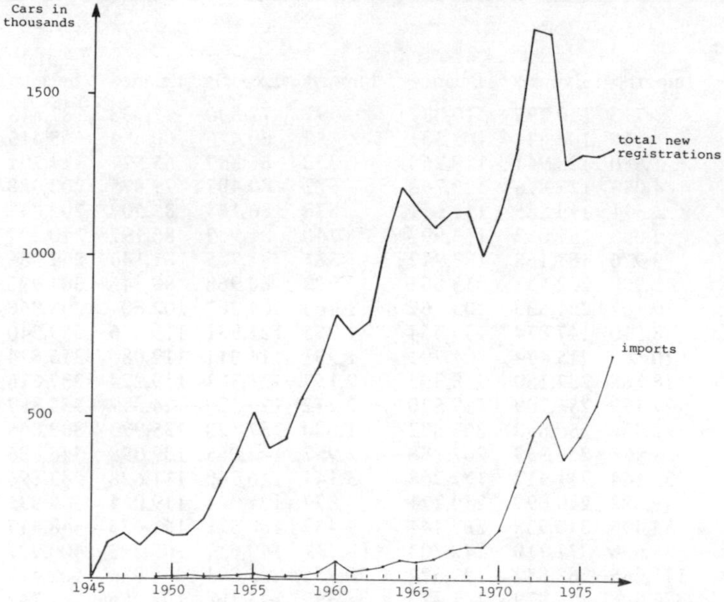

Source: SMMT

In the 1970s the long-run effects of government regulatory policy were clearly reflected in the balance of payments. In earlier chapters it was argued that government restraints increased exports in the short run but that a contrary influence on the balance of payments occurred in the long run. Squeezing the home market to force production to export markets reduced profit levels, so discouraging investment, research and development, the introduction of new designs and ultimately international competitiveness. Since 1948 the motor industry had been Britain's major export industry whilst, over the same period, car imports had been low. In the 1970s UK cars ceased in many respects to be internationally competitive, although they continued to be the nation's most important export. At the same time, and most importantly, import penetration of the British car market increased rapidly. By 1973 the balance of trade in cars, which for so many years had shown a healthy surplus, was just about in balance. The long-run consequences of a quarter of a century's use of the UK motor industry as an economic regulator had finally come home.

Table 6.5: UK Imports and Exports of Motor Vehicles, by Value, and Balance of Trade, 1952-77 (in £ thousands)

	Cars			CVs*			
Year	Imports	Exports	Balance	Imports	Exports	Balance	Total Balance
1952	713	110,795	110,082	97	77,830	77,733	187,815
1953	760	106,044	105,331	52	60,416	60,084	165,415
1954	1,680	120,944	119,264	332	65,859	65,527	184,791
1955	4,053	127,816	123,763	622	80,497	79,875	203,638
1956	2,344	119,885	117,541	638	86,145	85,507	203,048
1957	3,055	157,052	153,997	740	86,937	86,197	240,194
1958	3,926	187,168	183,242	581	81,725	81,144	264,986
1959	8,900	222,531	213,631	622	88,968	88,346	301,977
1960	19,101	224,633	205,562	1,463	104,267	102,804	308,366
1961	8,510	147,874	139,364	1,955	121,931	119,976	259,340
1962	10,680	215,474	204,794	1,931	114,011	112,080	316,874
1963	18,768	237,150	218,392	2,157	121,381	119,224	337,616
1964	27,139	256,709	229,570	2,212	126,529	124,317	353,887
1965	22,986	250,858	227,872	1,830	137,123	135,993	363,865
1966	26,567	234,355	207,788	2,957	142,055	139,098	346,886
1967	39,144	211,412	172,268	5,141	116,769	111,628	283,896
1968	49,328	280,099	230,771	5,877	124,941	119,064	349,835
1969	53,495	340,938	287,444	7,452	168,525	161,073	448,517
1970	85,006	327,710	242,704	13,389	179,612	166,223	408,927
1971	171,465	368,842	197,377	20,855	225,891	205,036	402,413
1972	324,406	329,879	5,473	38,899	175,168	136,269	141,742
1973	436,900	372,818	(64,082)	53,729	214,104	160,375	96,293
1974	355,005	418,502	63,497	91,141	250,082	158,941	222,438
1975	514,047	483,260	(30,787)	90,099	428,634	338,535	307,748
1976	886,397	633,230	(253,167)	122,725	548,204	425,479	172,312
1977	1,323,878	751,926	(571,952)	211,161	652,680	441,519	(130,433)

*Complete and chassis only

The instability of employment in the UK motor industry as a consequence of regulatory policy has been remarked upon on several occasions in this book. As the UK motor industry's viability as a leading sector came into question, and as its international competitiveness in an increasingly competitive world became doubtful, the many jobs dependent upon the industry were placed in jeopardy.

Export and Import Policy

In the seventies the nature of international trade for cars in Britain changed dramatically. Heath's expansionary policies of July 1971 signalled the end of the UK manufacturers' virtual monopoly of the home market and opened the door to increased imports. Further import penetration was encouraged by the reduction of tariffs on imported cars in 1972 to eleven per cent under the Kennedy Round agreements. Then, in 1973, Britain at last entered the European Economic Community. These moves provided opportunities for greatly increased international trade in cars. Unfortunately by this time UK producers were less able to exploit overseas markets than overseas manufacturers were able to exploit the British market, largely because of inadequate investment, an outdated model range and poor productivity improvement in the UK industry (see Table 6.5) over the previous decade. The rapid worsening of the balance of trade in cars spurred the government to protectionist measures. As, during 1974, imports from all countries, but particularly from Japan, increased, Sir Ray Brookes, President of the SMMT, solicited government help. At the summit meeting of world leaders at Rambouillet, France, in 1975, Mr Wilson obtained agreement for some limitation on imports to Britain. Then, later in 1975, the Trade Secretary, Mr Peter Shore, obtained a promise of voluntary restraint from the Japanese on car exports to Britain. This was despite the fact that Britain's case for protection from the Japanese was ostensibly weak. First, Britain's overall balance of trade with Japan in 1974 was in surplus. Secondly, British attempts to sell in Japan were poor. When, in 1974, Nissan offered BL space in its ships and the use of its dealers in Japan for after-sales service on BL cars, BL decided it could not produce enough cars to justify the arrangement. In addition, the agent in Japan for BL cars, Manibeni, was said to have to buy up BL cars in California and Hong Kong for reshipment to meet Japanese demand. On the other hand it was claimed, not only by the British, that the Japanese used non-tariff barriers such as anti-pollution requirements and controlled retail outlets to circumvent GATT agreements and hinder imports.[12] Still, Volkswagen exported many more cars to Japan than BL. In Britain the extent of the change in international trade over the previous five years was reflected by Nissan who outsold both Vauxhall and Chrysler, and by an overall import penetration rate of nearly 40 per cent. Thus, whilst between 1970 and 1975 imports increased sixfold, export levels hardly changed.

The stagnation of UK car exports as the UK motor industry became increasingly uncompetitive stimulated the government to direct action to help exports. Following the 1973 oil crisis, as all European countries attempted to increase trade to the Middle East, the Labour government made a major effort to help Chrysler (UK) obtain a £100 million contract to produce the outdated Hillman Hunter in Iran. This contract became effective in 1975 and was initially for five years.[13]

Effects on Basic Conditions

The dismal state of the UK motor industry in the seventies was reflected in the changed pattern of demand at home and abroad. Throughout the sixties imports had taken about six per cent of the domestic market. In February 1970 NEDO forecast that by 1975, as tariffs declined, the British motor industry should expect import penetration to rise to 15 per cent. Five months rather than five years later import penetration reached 15 per cent and five years later 40 per cent. Meanwhile, UK exports continued at about 30 per cent of production even though the other major car-producing countries in the EEC, France, Germany and Italy, exported over 50 per cent of production in 1975. The decline in popular demand for UK cars during these years was shown in a comparison of the American multinationals. In 1972 Chrysler (UK) exported 5,000 cars to Europe whilst Chrysler (France) exported 200,000; Ford (UK) and Vauxhall exports to Europe were about five per cent of those of Ford (Germany) and Opel. Worse still, Opel exported six times as many cars to the European Free Trade Area countries as Vauxhall. And whilst productivity at Opel had improved by 25 per cent since 1965, no improvement had occurred at Vauxhall. Value added at the German plants of GM and Ford was approximately double that of their British counterparts.[14] The low level of exports to the United States after 1971 resulted from a decision by all three American companies to source elsewhere than Britain because of poor quality.[15] Initially Ford and GM sourced entirely from Germany whilst Chrysler sourced from Mitsubishi in Japan. Though BL continued to export to North America it was 90 per cent reliant on its outdated range of sports cars. BL also exported the stodgy Austin Marina saloon there until 1975 when it ceased the effort because of poor consumer response even at bargain, dumped, prices.[16] By 1975 French, German, Italian, Japanese and Swedish cars outsold the once dominant British in North America. Overall, lower tariffs, EEC entry and some efforts at protection by the government did little to stem the considerable decrease in demand worldwide for the products of the UK motor industry in the first half of the seventies.

Table 6.6: 'Equivalent' Motor Vehicles Produced per Employee per Annum, 1955-76*

	UK	Germany	USA
1955	4.1	3.9	19.8
1965	5.8	6.4	25.0
1970	5.6	7.5	19.6
1973	5.8	7.7	25.0
1976	5.5	7.9	26.1

*Jones and Prais use the 'equivalent' method to weigh cars by size in order to get a fairer comparison of productivity

Source: D.T. Jones and S.J. Prais, 'Plant Size and Productivity in the Motor Industry: Some International Comparisons', *Oxford Bulletin of Economics and Statistics*, vol. 40 (May 1978), p. 142.

Effects on Structure

As productivity in the UK motor industry lagged behind that of European and Japanese producers, and as tariffs were lowered, so significant barriers to entry were removed in the early 1970s. This brought about a considerable change in industry structure. For the first time importers became significant in the domestic market and for the largest importers, such as Volkswagen and Nissan, market shares justified assembly plants in Britain. These would have been established had it not been for labour problems.[17] At the same time, by 1975, Vauxhall and Chrysler had experienced home market declines without a corresponding increase in exports. Thus both companies operated below capacity at production levels which failed to exploit potential economies of scale. As a result Chrysler made plans to run down its operations in Britain. Later these were changed when the British government intervened (see mergers section). Instead Chrysler (UK) was integrated more closely with Chrysler (France). GM decided to increase co-operation between Vauxhall and the larger German subsidiary Opel, although this went against GM's traditional policy of encouraging each group in the company to perform autonomously.

Effects on Conduct

Lower tariffs meant the ability of the UK motor industry to discriminate by price between the home and overseas market was markedly reduced. Even in Britain imports undersold the UK products by 1975; the cheapest car that year available in the UK was the Renault R4. Therefore, the domestic market ceased to be the captive lucrative market of bygone days. Even so, BL continued to sell cars below cost overseas and was found guilty of dumping the Austin Marina in the United States in 1975.

Lower tariffs in combination with the general decline in international competitiveness of the UK motor industry affected product strategy and product designs in 1974 and 1975. First, the Central Policy Review Staff (CPRS), among others, questioned whether BL should continue to produce mass-produced cars given the competitive superiority of the Japanese and Europeans and worldwide overcapacity in the industry. The CPRS suggested that BL might have more chance of export success and profitability by concentrating on its up-market executive saloons, Rovers and Jaguars, which could be competitive with BMW, Mercedes-Benz, Volvo and Peugeot. However, by 1975 the government had become directly involved in BL (see mergers section) and was concerned with other goals than mere profitability. A new range of BL mass-produced cars was therefore planned, not so much for export but as import substitutes. Secondly, at Vauxhall and Chrysler, the policy of producing distinct British designs was abandoned. In the future Chrysler (UK) would produce Chrysler (France) designs, whilst Vauxhall would produce essentially Opel designs.

Effects on Performance

Obviously the main consequence of tariff policy was on the balance of payments. Lower tariffs, at a time of greatly diminished UK international competitiveness, meant the balance of trade in cars deteriorated substantially. As imports grew more rapidly than exports, total demand for British cars suffered a relative decrease. This meant the UK motor manufacturers tended to operate at less than full capacity, with negative effects on efficiency, profits, progress and employment opportunities: the reverse effect of what EEC entry in 1963 would likely have achieved. Though specific policies to help exports, for example the Iran deal, and to reduce imports, for example the Rambouillet agreement, helped the balance of payments, government efforts to help the UK motor industry were too little and too late to clear up a situation for which twenty-five years of government mismanagement had been at least partly responsible.

Competitions Policy

Competitions policy is discussed below under two subheadings. The first

subheading is 'Mergers Policy'. This may be a misnomer for developments in the seventies since the changes in ownership which occurred
in the UK motor industry involved the government, but it is consistent
with the treatment of competitions policy in other chapters. Under a
second subheading 'Restrictive Trade Practices' are briefly examined.

Mergers Policy

Upon their election in 1970 the Conservative government had allowed
the Industrial Reorganisation Corporation, which had been instrumental
in the creation of BL, to lapse. In 1972 the Conservatives passed the
1972 Industrial Act to prevent a repeat of the elaborate parliamentary
procedure it had had to go through to save Rolls-Royce. The Act gave
the government powers to obtain an equity interest in private companies
and to provide financial aid on social and commercial grounds when the
City and other sources were unwilling to provide funds. When the Labour
Party was returned to office in 1974 they reintroduced the underlying
concept of the IRC when, in the Industry Bill, they proposed the setting
up of a National Enterprise Board (NEB). The NEB, established by the
1975 Industry Act, was instituted with powers to restructure apparently
healthy industries which might be in danger of failing. Comparable
bodies had been successful in Japan and France, whilst in Germany the
powerful banks had fulfilled a similar role.

The first industry to receive NEB restructuring finance was the motor
industry. The need for NEB assistance had its origins in the IRC-inspired
merger between BMH and Leyland to create BL in 1968. BL had proved
difficult to rationalise and by 1974 still offered six basic models, compared to four by the whole of Ford of Europe. On average only about
140,000 units of each model were produced annually, thus incurring a
considerable cost penalty and by 1974, as Table 6.7 shows, BL was at the
bottom of the productivity league for European volume car producers.
For 1973 BL had undertaken a major £500 million investment plan to
modernise, in an attempt to remedy this situation.[18] By sheer bad luck
these expenditures coincided with the unforeseeable fall in demand and
inflation following the OPEC oil crisis and the coalminers' strike. Given
the weak financial position of the firm, as a result of poor real profits
since the mid 1960s, BL found itself in a financial crunch. Their financial
crisis arose in part from accounting practices used at BL. For years depreciation had been inadequate, paper profits overstated and real capital
distributed in the form of dividends. These devices were used in order
to make BL apparently attractive to outsiders because, as Lord Stokes
said, justifying the approach, 'unless you are able to show some form

of return to investors then you are never able to excite them to put more money in'.[19] The government was approached for help. In return for guaranteeing BL's overdraft up to fifty million pounds, the government was given access to the company's financial records so that a report on its long-term prospects could be made. The report was made by Sir Donald Ryder, who was later appointed the first chairman of the NEB.

Table 6.7: Value Added per Man, 1974

GM (US)	£8,600
Ford (US)	7,966
Opel	5,875
Daimler-Benz	5,207
Volvo	4,886
Ford (Germany)	4,883
Volkswagen	4,767
Saab	4,637
Renault	4,133
Ford (UK)	3,901
Chrysler (UK)	2,765
Vauxhall	2,560
Fiat	2,259
BL	2,129

Source: Parliament (Commons), *Fourteenth Report of the Expenditure Committee, 1974-75: The Motor Vehicle Industry* (HMSO, London, 1975), p. 36.

The Ryder Report was not published in full because parts of it were libellous. Basically, on the strength of the Ryder Report, the government agreed to save the ailing company. Remedies had to be taken against the wide product range, overmanning and the effects of years of underinvestment. The Ryder Report estimated that, at current prices, nine hundred million pounds would have to be injected into the company between 1975 and 1978; five hundred million pounds as long-term loans, two hundred million pounds of government equity and two hundred million pounds in bank loans. Additionally, whilst the government was not to nationalise the company, it did offer to buy all existing shares at ten pence.[20] If all shareholders accepted the offer this would cost a further sixty million pounds. Then between 1978 and 1981 another five hundred million pounds would be needed. That meant that the total external cost of saving BL, in 1975 prices, was 1.3 billion pounds.

The Ryder Report recommended that none of BL's fifty-five factories be closed. The company would be reorganised into four groups. The largest would be cars. In addition, there would be international products, special products and trucks and buses. The Ryder Report's recommendations for structural reorganisation contradicted those of the managing director of BL, John Barber, who resigned. He had been hired from Ford following the creation of BL in 1968. Lord Stokes was effectively dismissed as chairman by an appointment to honorary president.

The Ryder Report said that without improved labour efficiency the company could not survive. Improved productivity would stem from cuts in the numbers of workers, greater movement and interchangeability between jobs and a reduction in the number of bargaining units. Ryder concluded that BL's success depended upon labour co-operation. If that was not forthcoming by 1978, Ryder recommended that further investment should be halted.

It is easy with hindsight to criticise the plan, but even at the time the government's total acceptance of the Ryder Report on how to save the remaining British owned car company received less than unanimous approval. First, critics argued that Ryder had been asked the wrong question. The government had asked Ryder, 'What was necessary to make BL profitable without financial restraint?' It was said he should have been asked, 'What was necessary to save BL?' For example, a think tank at Bristol University examined sixteen alternative programmes, including the Ryder scheme. They concluded that the Ryder approach would not generate profits in any case, and instead advocated a loss-minimising strategy.[21] Secondly, the Ryder Report was criticised for being hopelessly overoptimistic. The Trade and Industry subcommittee of the House of Commons believed that Ryder relied too much on BL's own forecasts about increased world penetration.[22] He also under-estimated required redundancies and gave 'a signal lack of supporting argument'[23] to the proposal that BL could compete with mass-produced cars.[24] Thirdly, the Ryder Report made stringent demands on labour; and as this book has repeatedly shown and many commentators pointed out at the time, the post-war history of labour co-operation with both government and management has been shaky to say the least.

Whilst the NEB was used to provide the financial requirements, Sir Ronald Edwards, a former head of the National Electricity Board and Professor of Industrial Organisation at London University, was appointed as chairman of BL with authority to implement the Ryder Report. This difficult task, which involved modernising BL and increasing home and world market penetration, was made no easier by a government decision late in 1975 to save Chrysler (UK).

Since acquiring Rootes in the mid-1960s, Chrysler had lost over four hundred million pounds in Britain. Quite simply Chrysler (UK), with an annual capacity of about 300,000 units, was too small. Twice in 1975 the government turned down requests from Chrysler (UK) for support similar to that initially given to BL in 1974. Furthermore, Chrysler did not qualify for help from the NEB since the NEB was 'charged to be commercially viable',[25] and by 1975 Chrysler (UK) clearly did not fall into such a category. In the first nine months Chrysler (UK) lost nearly one hundred million pounds. The parent company, itself in a parlous financial state, decided it must cut loose from Chrysler (UK) and told the British government 'that it would start liquidating Chrysler (UK) from the end of November . . . unless Her Majesty's government in the meantime took it over'.[26] Faced with what it called 'the fearsome choice' and 'with a pistol to their head',[27] the government quickly came to Chrysler's assistance. In addition to sharing losses of up to £72.5 million in order to give Chrysler the 'opportunity of viability', the government either provided or guaranteed ninety million pounds of loans.[28]

The government succumbed to Chrysler's gambit for two political reasons. First, the government wished to placate the Iranian government. In Iran, as a result of earlier government efforts, Chrysler (UK) had been permitted to build an assembly plant for knockdown car kits exported from Britain, and Iran, a large purchaser of UK armaments and engineering goods, let it be known that they did not want the assembly plant orphaned. Added support for the Iran influence stemmed from a loan of over one billion dollars from that country to Britain negotiated in 1974. Secondly, in 1974 it seemed quite possible that the Scottish Nationalists would split the Labour Party. If Chrysler was allowed to run down its UK operations, jobs in Scotland would be lost and, the government felt, so would vital Labour Party support. Financial aid to Chrysler made little economic sense.

Effects on Basic Conditions. The very context within which car demand was determined was modified by the direct interest which the government undertook with its involvement in BL and Chrysler (UK). As late as 1973 the government had used credit controls on the motor industry, despite its crippled status, to control the general level of aggregate demand following the energy crisis. After 1974 the government's capacity to use the motor industry as a regulatory policy tool was further constrained because of the effects of such policies on the viability of BL and Chrysler, and the higher level of visibility of the government's responsibility to, and association with, BL and Chrysler (UK). No longer was the government as able to create wide fluctuations in car demand to control aggregate demand heedless of the consequences.

On the supply side, a key element in the Ryder Report was the emphasis on improved labour co-operation. Yet one of the first comments made by the trade unions about the report was its failure to fulfil hopes of increased worker control and the feelings of alienation this created.[29] Whether these comments were serious is debatable. When the government offered Mr Jack Jones of the Transport and General Workers Union a position on the powerful four-man organising committee of the NEB, he declined. Similarly the trade unions turned down the offer of worker participation at Chrysler, including worker participation on the company board. The unions, who felt important decisions would still be made in Detroit anyway, had more sense than to take responsibility for sinking ships.[30]

In the administration of both the Ryder Report at BL and of financial aid to Chrysler (UK), trade union attitudes to labour co-operation were harmed. In December 1975, at BL, Ryder threatened to send the workers home if 28.5 cars per hour were not produced. The cars were not produced but when the management's bluff was called the workers were not sent home. Therefore, almost immediately, the government demonstrated its faint-heartedness, lost credibility and revealed itself to be no more capable than the old management at gaining labour co-operation. Trade union antagonism was also created during the negotiations of financial aid to Chrysler (UK). Admittedly the government was negotiating 'with a pistol to the head' and time was scarce, but their initial refusal to even talk to Chrysler shop stewards was myopic. In the event the shop stewards felt so aggrieved that they organised a sit-in at the House of Commons, after which Mr Varley, the Secretary of Employment, agreed to consult them. Once again, although the final outcome was in the workers' favour, the way in which government managed the situation had a negative effect on labour attitudes.

Effects on Structure. Given the size of the UK market there never had been room for all three US motor firms and BL in Britain. By the mid-1970s there was worldwide excess capacity in the motor industry. In addition, large expansions in Japan and Third World countries such as Korea and Brazil were underway. Ryder's belief that Britain could regain lost market shares internationally in the face of such competition was questionable from the beginning.[31] By maintaining Chrysler (UK) the government simply made the outlook for BL and Vauxhall, who the GM European manager had told in 1974, 'The oxygen is going out at such a rate you don't know how close to death you really are',[32] even

more difficult. Whilst it is likely that if Chrysler (UK) had been liquidated
many Chrysler (UK) dealers would have picked up import franchises
and that import penetration would have increased, market shares of BL,
Vauxhall and Ford would also have increased.[33]

Effects on Conduct. Since the 1960s over five hundred million pounds
of investment planned for the UK motor industry had been cancelled
because of inadequate profits.[34] In consequence, few new models had
been introduced and BL's and Chrysler (UK)'s model ranges in particular
were outdated. Infusions of government financial aid into the two companies enabled increased research, innovation and the development of a
new line of models. The purpose of these new designs was, it was hoped,
to make the companies profitable and, of at least equal importance to
the government, to act as import substitutes in the late 1970s and the
1980s.

Effects on Performance. The huge financial aid to BL and Chrysler (UK)
saved jobs in the UK motor industry and clearly slowed the rate of
growth of import penetration. In considering the effects on the country's
economic goals, notably full employment and the balance of payments,
but also on economic growth, equity and the allocation of resources,
the opportunity cost of financial aid to the UK motor industry must be
considered. In 1972 the government claimed it would 'back winners' in
the UK motor industry.[35] Ford (UK), who between 1964 and 1975
made profits of about two hundred million pounds, about the same as
Chrysler (UK)'s losses, must have wondered what happened to *their*
financial aid. From its track record Ford could have used the financial
aid more efficiently than BL or Chrysler (UK) to help maintain full
employment and contribute to the balance of payments. By the same
token so might other industries such as micro-electronics, chemicals,
armaments or even commercial vehicles or the motor components industry, all of which showed a greater ability to operate efficiently and
competitively than motor industry lame ducks. In the previous thirty
years hundreds of thousands of jobs had been lost in mining, textiles,
agriculture, ship building and rail transport and more would be lost in
those industries in the future. There was little economic justification
for treating BL and Chrysler (UK) as special cases.

Employment and the balance of payments were the justification for
financial aid to try and make BL and Chrysler (UK) viable. These matters
deserve further consideration. If BL had been allowed to decline the
import share of the British market would have increased considerably.

However, the effect on Britain's balance of payments would have been so great that Britain would probably have had to establish some sort of tariff rebate system similar to the Canadian-United States auto pact. (Under this pact a US car importer to Canada gets rebates on tariffs if they purchase components in Canada.) Britain's components industry had proved to be internationally competitive. Therefore, if BL had declined it is possible that the components industry would have grown more rapidly, had some sort of tariff rebate system been introduced to offset partially or totally the negative effects on employment and the balance of payments. The decision to save Chrysler, which made BL's task of becoming internationally competitive more difficult, was made on the grounds of its effect on employment. The government claimed that financial aid to Chrysler would save 25,000 jobs at Chrysler and a further 25,000 jobs in related industries.[36] The claim was made on the assumption that no new jobs would become available for the released labour, and that all indirectly dependent jobs would be lost as well. This was despite the fact that less than one thousand Chrysler workers lived at Linwood. The majority commuted from Paisley and Johnstone where the unemployment rate of five per cent was less than the national average and the Midlands rate. Even so, support for Chrysler could not save jobs overall. If Britain was to become internationally competitive, the labour force in the motor industry had to decline. Maintaining Chrysler simply put more pressure on an already hard-pressed BL. Labour resources had to be squeezed out of the motor industry in the long run. This would occur over time either as uncompetitive firms closed their doors or as increasingly efficient firms raised productivity to international levels. For the short run, the consequences of financial aid to BL and Chrysler (UK) as regards employment and the balance of payments were positive and, more importantly, politically expedient.

Restrictive Trade Practices

In the seventies the Monopolies Commission continued to have minimal impact on the UK motor industry although one interesting, if insignificant, development concerning firm conduct occurred in 1972. By that time it was widely accepted that quality control was generally superior in Germany, Sweden, the Benelux countries and Japan than in Britain. In the Fair Trading Act 1973 the government established a new Monopolies Commission which had powers of reference which included the ability to deal with complaints about low quality. However, since each individual case for examination still had to be authorised by the Minister it was little more than window dressing and had no significant effect on the UK motor industry.

Labour Relations

Over the decade to 1970 labour relations in the UK, and in the UK motor industry in particular, had become increasingly unsatisfactory. Government regulatory policy and attempts at labour reform in the 1960s had been partly responsible for this deterioration. Undaunted by the previous Labour government's efforts at reform, the newly elected Conservative government came to power in 1970 with a mandate to put labour relations into a legal framework with legally enforceable contracts. The 1971 Industrial Relations Bill sought to end unofficial strikes, introduce legally binding contracts and ban closed shops. It attempted to obtain a transfer of power from the shop stewards to the union officials. To achieve these goals the Act offered the unions a number of legal privileges, notably greater access to information relevant to bargaining, in return for registering with a Registrar of Trade Unions. No compulsion was involved. The Conservative government intended the privileges of registration to act as an incentive to registration and hoped, falsely, that labour relations reform would come about as a result of a voluntary trade union response to incentives. But at the 1971 Trades Union Congress a vote not to register was passed, albeit by only a small majority. Obviously within the trade union movement a large section was in favour of reform even though the majority saw the Industrial Relations Bill as an attack on hard-earned privileges. In the motor industry opposition to the new legislation made 1971 the worst year for labour relations since the General Strike and over three million working days were lost.[37] Within the motor industry labour relations were also hampered between 1971 and 1972 by the government's incomes policy. This policy, introduced at a time when the industry was still converting from a piecework to a measured day work system, hindered the establishment of a rational pay structure for motor industry workers.

In 1974, when a minority Labour government was returned to power they repealed the Industrial Relations Act as promised. Legally labour relations were returned to the same basis as had existed before 1971, though it was hoped they would be improved by the Social Contract. The Social Contract was an agreement between the unions and the Labour government. The spirit of the agreement was that the unions would only put in for wage claims to keep pace with the cost of living. Almost immediately the contract was put to the test. Early in September 1974 a strike at Ford's Dagenham plant in support of a wage claim in excess of the Social Contract occurred. This placed the government in an awkward position. Whilst Mr Jack Jones, leader of TGWU, attempted to make the contract hold, at least until the coming election, the Labour government blamed the strike on the previous Conservative government's incomes policy. Mr Michael Foot, the Secretary of State and Employment, said that 'one of the difficulties of Fords [sic] and elsewhere are the injustices and anomalies left over by that statutory incomes policy . . .'[38] However, in fact the Social Contract was inadequate to the task of dealing with Britain's labour relations problems and inflation. Not even all the trade unions supported it. In the AEU journal Mr Hugh Scanlon, leader of the Amalgamated Engineering Union, wrote, 'The social compact is not really a compact at all . . . inflation must be solved but this will never be achieved by wage restraint . . . We very much regretted that the debate on the social compact should have taken place at all.'[39]

Effects on Basic Conditions

Several factors were important in explaining the increasingly hostile and damaging labour relations scenario of the UK motor industry in the 1970s which largely affected basic conditions and attitudes. The effects of earlier government regulatory policy in creating what the Fourteenth Report of the Expenditure Committee called 'insecurity and uncertainty' have already been discussed.[40] No doubt increased import penetration after 1970 aggravated these fears. Three further developments were also important. First, attempts to place labour relations on a legal basis were like a red flag to a bull in that they provided fertile ground for the more militant elements in the labour movement to create industrial strife. Secondly, the labour relations system as it existed was incapable of handling the inflationary situation that developed in the 1970s. Thirdly, since the sixties a decrease in the concept of brotherhood and an increase in self-centredness allowing hostile factions to develop within the labour movement occurred. Some specific examples illustrate these points.

In 1971 a huge strike took place at Ford during the passage of the Industrial Relations Bill. By this time Ford was the only really profitable car firm left in the UK; despite 155 strikes and eleven overtime bans in 1970. The strike ostensibly was over a pay dispute, but the media reported that the strike was as much against the Conservative government's labour relations reform proposals as against Ford. Ford quickly agreed to trade union demands, but upon condition of a twelve-month grading standstill. The unions rejected the offer and there was a deadlock. By the seventh week over 100,000 vehicles worth over seventy

million pounds had been lost. Still the strike dragged on for a further
four weeks before a settlement was made, during which time it was
apparent that further stoppages could provide no financial benefits to
the unions and that emotion had got the upper hand of economic
rationality. This prolonged strike also harmed business attitudes. In a
letter to *The Times* Henry Ford II announced that Ford had scrapped
investment plans for a new £30 million engine plant in Britain which
would have produced the engines for the North American Ford Pinto.
Following discussions with the Prime Minister, Mr Ford commented 'the
labour situation has got to be cleaned up otherwise our customers will
go elsewhere'.[41] Management-labour relations had sunk to new levels.

The inadequacy of the UK motor industry's industrial relations
system to handle the growing problems of inflation stemmed in part
from the fact that in the industry, particularly where the measured day
work system had not been introduced and there was still piecework,
there was a myriad of different wage agreements. Facing up to twenty
unions in seventy factories BL, for example, made new wage agreements
daily. As inflationary expectations created a further variable in negotiations, historical parities became increasingly difficult to maintain. Each
new inflationary settlement tarnished the satisfaction given by the
previous one to a different group. Inflation, therefore, served to aggravate other problems already existing in the factories: thus, as inflation
began to spiral upwards in the seventies so did labour problems. With
up to four hundred accredited shop stewards in a factory, often with a
left-wing bias, there was plenty of scope for justifying work stoppages.
Although by 1970 Ford, Vauxhall and Chrysler had gone over to a day
rate pay system, BL still had 134,000 workers on piecerate.[42] Increasingly too, difficulties arose from components suppliers who still operated
on piecework. Management in the car factories complained bitterly that
shortages of supplies because of strikes hampered day-to-day operations
and were the norm rather than the exception.[43]

In 1970 a number of strikes occurred which reflected the interacting
problems of a poor labour relations system, a lack of brotherhood, and
inflation. One of these was at a large components supplier, GKN-Sankey,
who manufactured car wheels. There, five thousand men asked for a
weekly rise of eight pounds and ten shillings, about twenty per cent.
The management resisted the inflationary demands. Within four weeks
over one third of the total UK motor industry's labour force was laid
off and BL's Standard-Triumph division was completely closed. Commenting on the strike at a TUC meeting Mr Vic Feather, leader of the
TUC, noted that 'One man's strike means another man's lay-off.'[44] Still,

the GKN workers were prepared to hold off for a fifth week when GKN management, under enormous pressure from the car manufacturers, yielded to the strikers' demands. The five thousand GKN workers got their wage increase but at a huge cost to themselves, other motor industry workers and the UK economy.

One outcome of this sort of strike was demands by the unions for guaranteed pay when stoppages occurred because of strikes in other factories.[45] These agreements added to the anarchy in the labour relations system. Workers with a guaranteed wage put less pressure on their striking 'brothers' to return to work. In effect, it meant that the employers often subsidised unofficial strikes.[46]

The havoc caused by an out-of-control labour relations system was well demonstrated by a strike at Chrysler (UK) in 1973.[47] It began when the Ryton plant was shut down because of a strike at another Chrysler plant. Upon their recall to Ryton the workers found that parts of the cars were 'shoddy', so that eventually the line had to be shut down and the men sent home again. The dispute arose whether the men should be paid for a ninety minute period when the line did not operate. It was a question of whether the men or the parts were at fault. One foreman said,

> I was responsible for the panels coming in from Linwood, and they were not up to scratch. It makes it very difficult for the foreman when he puts a tab on a car for quality and management nips it off. The foreman has no face . . .[48]

Foremen are part of management. The chaos caused by strikes had undermined management-management relations as well as labour relations. The unofficial Ryton strike was further aggravated when the Chrysler (UK) managing director, Mr Geoffrey Hunt, threatened that until labour relations improved no further investment in the United Kingdom would be made. Eventually, in contradiction to earlier ultimatums, the management agreed to talk to the strikers' *unofficial* leaders. This reflected the fact that official procedures had not worked in this case as they had seemed unable to do in so many others. Finally, after five weeks and making headline news, the management decided it could not identify the workers responsible for the shoddy work and therefore agreed to pay them for the lost ninety minutes of production.

The Ryton strike was big enough to inspire a long debate in the House of Commons about the 'growing conflict in the motor industry'.[49] The motion requested 'a full and independent inquiry into labour relations in the industry'.[50] Although the motion failed, the debate provided some useful insights. One of these was to the effect that labour relations reform might be a necessary but not sufficient condition for the restoration of industrial sanity. Perhaps Britain, quite simply, was an unsuitable place to produce cars. In Japan, Brazil and Spain the recent memory of poverty was sufficient to outweigh the tedium of work on the production lines.[51] And whilst nobody in the debate made the point, the labour force in Germany, France, Italy and the USA had similar characteristics. All the European car factories employed many 'guest' workers from Southern Europe and North Africa, whilst much of the labour on Detroit's production lines were first-generation black immigrants from the South. Therefore they too had often had a first-hand experience of real poverty. The alienating boredom of the work, reminiscent of the movie *Modern Times* made by Charlie Chaplin as long ago as 1940, was brought out in a letter to *The Times* by the former managing director of Chrysler (UK), Mr George Cattell. He said,

> Men were engaged on repetitive operations with a 1.6 minute cycle for eight hours a day, five days a week, with little interest in what they were doing and little prospect of change. I know from experience that the very monotony gave rise to unreasonable and uncooperative attitudes.[52]

By the seventies, labour relations had become impossible. Not only were labour-management relations in chaos and management-shop floor relations weak, but labour-labour relations were in disarray. In 1973 a number of rebellions against militant union leaders occurred. In February 1973 a meeting held by the conveners at Ford to realise a desired strike vote failed. In the same week the men at Ford's Dagenham plant voted to call off an overtime ban.[53] These events sufficiently impressed Henry Ford II that he announced that his confidence had been restored in the British Ford workers.[54] The same sort of thing happened again in May when the national negotiating committee of the eighteen unions at Ford called for a strike against Ford's wage offer on the basis of reassurances from the shop stewards that there was wide support among the members for such a strike. However, when local newspapers balloted the men they found four out of five were against strike action and a strike vote against strike action was taken.[55] At the same time management let it be known that they had received requests from workers for secret ballots because their own elected shop floor representatives would not allow them to have them. Opposition among the moderates to perpetual strike activity was also seen in 1974 at the BL Cowley works. In April about 12,000 workers were laid off over a dispute about lay-off pay. BL decided to take the opportunity of low market demand to rid itself of an unpopular Trotskyist shop steward, a Mr Alan Thornett, chairman of the joint shop stewards' committee. Before any action in support of Thornett had taken place the wives of the Cowley workers arrived at the factory gates in support of the BL management.[56] They, they said, were fed up with the perpetual strikes at Cowley, often over political matters, which had cost them, the Cowley housewives, ten pounds per week since the beginning of the year. This support enabled the moderates to prevent a strike. However, these examples of anti-militant revolts were exceptions to the generally strike-torn environment of labour relations in the motor industry in the early seventies. For the most part the more active, aggressive and militant factions continued to rule the day. Though the cases at Ford and BL related above reveal that there was considerable support for labour relations reform to create a less chaotic system, the problem was that the government was unable to identify with and use that support to achieve successful labour relations reform.[57]

Effects on Structure

The failure of government labour relations reform to improve the situation in the UK motor industry had some effect on structure. First, Chrysler as well as Ford cut back on announced investment plans in the UK, and nobody knows what other plans were quietly shelved. Secondly, Volkswagen decided not to open up a plant in Britain 'because of labour troubles and economic uncertainties',[58] despite the fact that by 1970 the hourly rates for skilled labour were well below German rates. Thirdly, costs increased. In 1975 the SMMT estimated that a car company in the UK exporting 40 per cent of production broke even at about seventy per cent of capacity.[59] They also estimated that in 1972 ten per cent, in 1973 twenty per cent, and in 1974 twenty-six per cent of potential (full capacity) car production was lost and not recovered as a result of industrial disputes inside and outside the industry.[60] Furthermore, the SMMT saw this as the 'tip of the iceberg'.[61] In other countries one big strike could cause many working days to be lost, but could be planned for. In the UK hundreds of minor, unforeseen and unrecorded strikes in the motor companies and components suppliers created a constant and costly disruption of production schedules which seriously eroded profitability. To handle this problem in the seventies, the motor firms adopted two precautionary policies. The first policy was to make 'crippled' cars. Whenever necessary, and if possible, cars were produced without unavailable components. These parts were then fitted later, when available. Production scheduling became largely a matter of improvisation. The second policy adopted by the motor firms was dual sourcing. At considerable additional cost, two suppliers of vital components were kept, so that if one supplier should go on strike, the other could keep the production lines moving.[62]

Effects on Conduct

Obviously labour relations problems meant lower productivity and higher costs, and were one factor responsible for the rapid rise in car prices between 1970 and 1975. Also, fear of labour opposition, aggravated by the piecework system where it still applied, discouraged the improvement of production processes, the modification of existing designs, the introduction of new designs or any change at all. Labour resistance was one reason among many for the slow pace at which the much-needed rationalisation of BL model range proceeded. Finally, poor quality, in part attributable to poor labour relations, was one justification given by Ford, Vauxhall and Chrysler to cease exports from Britain to the USA in 1971 and instead source from Germany and Japan.

Effects on Performance

The overall performance objectives of the economy were manifestly harmed by poor labour relations. Production, exports, home market shares, profits and foreign investment were all reduced with clear consequences on economic growth, allocative efficiency and the balance of payments. In 1974 about 450,000 cars were irrevocably lost through industrial disputes and about 350,000 cars imported.[63] By the 1970s demand worldwide for cars had become increasingly homogeneous and essentially similar global cars such as the Ford Escort and Cortina, the GM Chevette, the VW Golf, the Datsun Cherry and the Toyota Corolla were sold in many markets. Consequently, observed Vauxhall's chairman Mr David Hegland, 'so long as strikes interrupt production and delay delivery of British cars, imported cars will fill the gap'.[64]

Taxation Policy

In April 1973 a major revision of the system of indirect taxation was made in the UK when Value Added Tax (VAT) replaced purchase tax and the Selective Employment Tax (SET). The purchase tax on cars of 25 per cent was replaced by a VAT of 19.2 per cent on cars. Since purchase tax had been levied on wholesale prices whilst the VAT was levied on retail prices it was estimated that an 18 per cent VAT was approximately equivalent to the old purchase tax.[65] After taking account of trade-in prices and discounts it meant there was little change in the final price paid by consumers on new cars. At the same time the running costs of cars increased slightly since VAT applied to spare parts and servicing costs whose price rose more by virtue of VAT than they fell from the removal of SET. Despite the revision of the tax system the annual road fund car licence duty was retained on all cars at twenty-five pounds. Although this was approximately half the 1948 rate in real terms, it still brought in over five hundred million pounds to the Exchequer[66] (see Table 6.8).

Table 6.8: Estimated Receipts by Central Government from UK Road Users, 1961-77 (£ millions)

Year	Fuel Tax	Road Fund Vehicle Licence	Total excluding Purchase Tax	Purchase Tax on cars, motorcycles and chassis	Car Tax	Value Added Tax	Total
1961	383	134	517	160			677
1962	431	156	587	149			736
1963	461	172	633	119			752
1964	529	184	713	146			859
1965	660	228	888	144			1032
1966	724	258	982	146			1128
1967	806	277	1083	169			1252
1968	926	371	1297	208			1505
1969	1092	416	1508	210			1718
1970	1171	436	1607	256			1863
1971	1232	450	1682	325			2007
1972	1296	471	1767	362			2129
1973	1408	499	1907	101	81	105	2194
1974	1352	505	1857		124	152	2133
1975	1386	679	2065		179	700	2944
1976	1840	778	2618		224	660	3502
1977	2156	693	2849		274	710	4111

Sources: SMMT; Dept of Transport.

Consequences of Taxation Policy

By adding a special car tax to the standard rate of VAT, the new tax was approximately equivalent to the old purchase tax on cars and therefore little change in new car prices resulted. The increase in running costs of older cars may have caused a small increase in new car demand. Rebates on VAT paid on exports meant no effect on overseas prices. Finally, by maintaining the road fund car licence at a flat rate, discrimination was continued against the small car and against the private owner who typically drives fewer miles a year than a businessman. Abolishment of the flat rate duty and a higher rate of VAT on petrol to compensate for tax losses would have redressed this situation but the opportunity was not taken. One reason for this was that the UK motor industry by 1973 was particularly uncompetitive in the area of small cars and replacing the road fund licence by a higher VAT on petrol would have encouraged more small car sales and hence yet higher levels of imports. Of course discouraging small-car development and purchase had been the original intention of the flat rate duty when instituted in 1948 in order to encourage the production and exports of larger cars. Ironically, and reflecting how things had changed in twenty-five years, it was maintained after 1973 to discourage imports. Overall VAT considerably altered relative prices within the UK economy, but its effect on the motor industry was small.

Transport and Environmental Policies

Previous chapters paid considerable attention to the transport policies of different governments. It was argued that in the post-war era too much emphasis was placed on the railways whilst inadequate expenditures were made on the roads with harmful consequences for UK designs and industry export performance. By the 1970s this had changed. During the sixties the car had been accepted as the inevitable dominant form of private transport and road expenditures, including the building of motorways, had increased rapidly. This meant that by 1970 the UK had the framework of a modern road system similar to those in other industrialised countries and so no longer needed special designs appropriate to different driving conditions. The global car, whether produced in the UK or elsewhere, was quite suitable. Thus, although during the seventies the motorway system was expanded and improved, it was the building of the first thousand miles in the 1960s which was most responsible for the change in design requirements.

Summary

At the beginning of 1970 there were few readily visible signs of how close the UK motor industry was to disaster. Although the cancer of inadequate investment, poor productivity, worsening labour relations and fragmented structure had been undermining the industry for years, it took Heath's abortive 'dash for growth' policy, EEC entry and lower tariffs, and the energy crisis between 1971 and 1973, to trigger the fall. Then, despite a number of government white papers and inquiries, investigations by a number of other private and public bodies and much discussion by the media, it seemed too late to remedy the situation. By 1975 the government was pouring aid into BL and Chrysler (UK), imports had taken over 40 per cent of the market, Vauxhall had lost its autonomy and become a minor partner to Opel, and only Ford could be called, by any stretch of the imagination, successful. As the industry's international weaknesses became clear, the government was compelled to abandon the frequent use of the industry as an economic regulator, as it had so used it in the past. Indeed, between 1970 and 1975 the government was reduced to trying to protect the industry from overseas competition. Meanwhile, the commitment to road transport made in the 1960s meant expenditures on the road system continued at historically high levels.

Notes

1. *The Economist*, 2 Oct. 1971, p. 74.
2. Ibid., 17 Feb. 1973, p. 80.
3. *Financial Times*, 20 Feb. 1974.
4. Central Policy Review Staff, *The Future of the British Car Industry* (HMSO, London, 1975), p. 68.
5. Ibid., p. 67.
6. Parliament (Commons), *Fourteenth Report from the Expenditure Committee, 1974-75: The Motor Vehicle Industry* (HMSO, London, 1975), p. 407.
7. Ibid., p. 413.
8. Parliament (Commons), *The Regeneration of British Industry*, Command 3710 (HMSO, London, 1974).
9. Ibid., para. 6.
10. Parliament (Commons), *Motor Vehicle Industry*, p. 409.
11. An excellent discussion of management weaknesses at BL is to be found in E.A. Salmon, 'Inside British Leyland', *Management Today*, 114 (Nov. 1975), pp. 59-61.
12. W.C. Duncan, *US-Japan Auto Diplomacy: A Study in Economic Confrontation* (Ballinger, Cambridge, Mass., 1973), p. 86.
13. *The Economist*, 11 Jan. 1975, p. 75.
14. Central Policy Review Staff, *The Future of the British Car Industry*, p. 81.
15. *The Economist*, 2 Feb. 1971, p. 86.
16. Ibid., 8 May 1976, p. 97.
17. See p. 145.
18. Parliament (Commons), *British Leyland: The Next Decade* (HMSO, London, 1975), p. 11.
19. Parliament (Commons), *Motor Vehicle Industry*, p. 99.
20. Parliament (Commons), *British Leyland*, p. 10.
21. *The Economist*, Oct. 1975, p. 79.
22. In 1952 BMC had been the world's fourth largest producer of motor vehicles. In 1975 it was the twelfth largest. It had been outranked by such companies as VW, Renault, Fiat, Toyota and Nissan.
23. Parliament (Commons), *Motor Vehicle Industry*, p. 196.
24. Given the UK motor industry's relative decline since 1945, it seemed all

too likely that massive investment would simply keep the industry one step behind the Japanese and Europeans in the highly competitive mass-produced car market.

25. Parliament (Commons), *Eighth Report of the Expenditure Committee, 1975-76: Public Expenditure on Chrysler (UK)* (HMSO, London, 1976), p. 18.

26. *The Listener*, Sept. 1974.

27. HCD, 6 Nov. 1975, col. 607.

28. Parliament (Commons), *Public Expenditure on Chrysler*, p. 93.

29. Ibid.

30. Parliament (Commons), *Motor Vehicle Industry*, p. 76.

31. Ibid., p. 93.

32. *The Economist*, 23 Feb. 1974, p. 94.

33. Parliament (Commons), *Public Expenditure on Chrysler*, p. 105.

34. Parliament (Commons), *Motor Vehicle Industry*, p. 424.

35. *Sunday Times*, 9 June 1979.

36. Parliament (Commons), *Public Expenditure on Chrysler*, p. 79.

37. Parliament (Commons), *Motor Vehicle Industry*, p. 404.

38. *The Listener*, Sept. 1974.

39. *The Economist*, 21 Sept. 1974, p. 111.

40. Parliament (Commons), *Motor Vehicle Industry*, p. 76.

41. *The Times*, 24 Feb. 1971.

42. *The Economist*, 'Survey of the Motor Industry', 17 Oct. 1970.

43. Ibid.

44. *The Economist*, 12 Sept. 1970, p. 77.

45. The insecurity of the workers about strikes was reflected in the desire to obtain financial support during a strike over and above state aid. A laid-off worker received over fifty per cent of his pay after three weeks from the state. If working conditions had been more stable, it seems reasonable to believe the unions would have pressed for different benefits.

46. Men on unofficial strike received no strike pay from the union.

47. The development of events during the Ryton strike revealed the poor state of British labour relations. Chrysler had had forty-two strikes that year and there must have been more clear issues than 'shoddy' parts with which to challenge the unions. Nevertheless the managing director of Chrysler (UK), Mr Geoffrey Hunt, threatened the workers that unless labour relations improved there would be no further investment in Britain. In response to this statement picket lines were strengthened. Management continued to pour salt on sore wounds. At the Stoke engine plant, which was picketed in sympathy with Ryton, the management decided to get an independent haulage company to take the engines out through a piece of fence purposely broken for that procedure. This was despite the fact that it would have been quite legal to have crossed the picket upon explanation of the purpose. In any event, the pickets discovered what was happening, fighting broke out, and a man on the pickets suffered a broken pelvis. Management then went against official procedure, had talks with the men on the unofficial strike, therefore acknowledging them, and agreed not to cross the picket lines. Finally, after five weeks and making headline news, the management decided it could not identify the workers responsible for the shoddy work. It therefore agreed to pay them for the lost ninety minutes of production.

48. *The Economist*, 19 June 1973, p. 71.

49. HCD, 25 June 1973, col. 1136.

50. Ironically the debate nearly did not occur. W. Price MP, who moved the motion, had his British car 'blow up' on the way to the debate. A lorry driver gave him a lift.

51. HCD, 25 June 1973, col. 1143.

52. *The Times*, 8 June 1973.

53. *The Times*, 22 Feb. 1973.

54. Ibid.

55. *Daily Telegraph*, 10 May 1973.

56. *Daily Telegraph*, 27 Apr. 1974.

57. The decline of the British motor industry has frequently been blamed on poor labour relations. Some alternative, if less popular, arguments can also be made about labour relations. First, poor management may have had an important effect on labour relations. For example, the unions have criticised the competence of management in getting parts to the production line. In British industry as a whole, unions complain of long periods of idleness because necessary parts are not available. This is management's responsibility. Secondly, low productivity in Britain has been blamed on low investment. In turn, low investment has been blamed on labour friction. However, it may equally well be that poor management and low investment were a cause of low productivity. As worker expectations of higher wages comparable to those in Europe were frustrated, labour relations deteriorated. Finally, when things go wrong in the UK motor industry it is all too easy to blame labour relations for poor performance.

58. *The Economist*, 'Survey of the Motor Industry', 17 Oct. 1970.

59. Parliament (Commons), *Motor Vehicle Industry*, p. 435.

60. Ibid., p. 432.

61. Ibid., p. 423.

62. Dual sourcing affected the structure and performance of the components supply industry. It called forth additional sources of supply domestically and in addition there was an increase in sourcing from abroad.

63. Parliament (Commons), *Motor Vehicle Industry*, pp. 399 and 432.

64. *The Economist*, 10 Aug. 1970, p. 45.

65. D. Johnstone, *A Tax Shall be Charged* (HMSO, London, 1972), p. 108.

66. *The Economist*, 13 Jan. 1977, p. 50.

7 RECENT DEVELOPMENT: STARTING AGAIN IN A NEW ORDER, 1976-79

In 1978 the Governor of the Bank of England said, 'the conventional methods of demand management can only work well against a background of financial stability. In recent years the economic system has received so many shocks that the stability of the post-war world has been fractured.'[1] Following the breakdown of the Bretton Woods system of fixed exchange rates early in the seventies, the government found the old tools of regulatory policy were less effective. To combat inflation and high unemployment the Labour government stressed other approaches after 1975. There was more reliance on monetary policy and income controls, whilst industrial strategies were used in an attempt to improve the supply side of the economy. These new approaches held different consequences for the motor industry. Whereas often in the past, demand management regulatory policy had particularly emphasised the motor industry, the use of incomes and monetary policies did not. On the other hand, industrial strategy programmes had considerable direct effects on the industry. So did government efforts to influence international trade. In addition, the government affected the industry through taxation, transport, regional and environmental policies.

Regulatory Policy

Changed circumstances and changed attitudes characterised government regulatory policy after 1976. Changed circumstances imposed constraints on the government's ability to use the motor industry as part of regulatory policy. Changed attitudes modified their desire to do so.

In prior years, when the UK car industry had been healthier, the government had exploited it, as earlier chapters showed, as a policy instrument to 'fine tune' aggregate demand and to influence the balance of payments. By 1976 a less competitive industry made such policy impractical. Encouraging car demand in Britain only tended to pull in more imports, whilst abroad British designs were, by and large, uncompetitive. In any case by 1976 the Labour government had become disillusioned with the neo-Keynesian demand management policies followed by both political parties since 1945. From 1976 James Callaghan and his now conservative Chancellor of the Exchequer, Denis Healey, followed a monetarist strategy which included restraints on government spending

152

and a declaration that inflation, which ran at almost thirty per cent in 1975, not unemployment, which approached 1.5 million in 1976, was the country's main enemy. This dramatic change in government policy was spurred on by a critical run on sterling in 1976 following three years of awesome balance of payments deficits and budget deficits.

Table 7.1: UK Visible Balance of Trade, 1952-77 (£ millions)

1952	−279
53	−244
54	−204
55	−313
56	+ 53
57	− 29
58	+ 29
59	−117
60	−406
61	−152
62	−102
63	− 80
64	−519
65	−237
66	− 73
67	−567
68	−682
69	−172
70	− 42
71	−1261
72	−722
73	−2383
74	−5235
75	−3236
76	−3589
77	−1709

As a condition for a three billion dollar credit from the IMF, the government agreed in a letter of intent to the IMF to set modest annual growth targets for the money supply as well as budgetary ceilings for both central and local government, in order to 'maintain stability in the exchange markets consistent with the maintenance of UK manufactures both at home and overseas'.[2]

From 1976 until 1979 the major planks of government regulatory policy, in addition to the money growth targets and government spending restraints mentioned above, were price controls and the Social Contract. Whilst these policies had less direct influence on the motor industry than earlier demand management policies, they did have serious repercussions.

Effects on Basic Conditions

The success accompanying Stage One and Stage Two of the government's Social Contract between July 1975 and June 1977 meant a dramatic drop in real incomes. Indeed, during Stage Two real average earnings fell by eight per cent, making the largest fall in real income for over one hundred years. Whilst the inflation rate declined by nearly one half from its 1975 high, real economic growth was negligible in 1976 and 1977. As a result the demand for cars in the UK was restrained. Still, despite falling real incomes, a number of factors meant some recovery in car demand in 1976 and 1977 as compared to the awful post-OPEC-crisis years. First, in order to circumvent Stages One and Two of the government's pay policy, many firms offered company cars in lieu of pay increases or higher salaries. For example, such jobs as chartered accountants, necessitating limited travel, often advertised a free car as a part of the job: in 1976 the British Institute of Management estimated that one third of all new cars were bought by companies.[3] Secondly, pent-up demand from 1974 and 1975 increased demand for cars in 1976 and 1977. Demand for cars was also stimulated in 1977 when the Control of Hiring Order 1977 was issued. Previously a deposit equal to ten monthly rentals had to be made when a car was leased on a long-term basis. In 1977 the deposit was reduced to three months, so opening up the whole vehicle leasing field; in 1979 the capital allowance on leased cars was reduced from 100 per cent to 25 per cent making leasing less attractive to companies for tax purposes, but saving the government £175 million.

After 1975 the UK motor industry got the more stable demand conditions it had long asked for. The government ceased to change credit conditions affecting car demand in order to manipulate aggregate demand. In 1975 the Treasury admitted that in the past it had under-estimated the negative consequences of such policies on the motor industry. Unfortunately by 1976 the main beneficiaries were as much the foreign manufacturers as the British.

Effects on Structure

As during the Social Contract rampant inflation came under some control, so Britain became a more attractive place to invest. Low wages, political stability, an efficient transport system and a common language were cited as reasons for the choice of Wales for Ford's £180 million engine plant[4] (see Table 7.2).

Table 7.2: Gross Hourly Wages in Motor Industry, by Country, 1978

United States	$ 8.65
West Germany	5.65
Japan	4.30
France	3.50
United Kingdom	3.45
Italy	2.90
Mexico	2.05
South Korea	0.80
Brazil	0.60
Philippines	0.35

Source: *The Economist*, 10 June 1978, p. 92.

Nevertheless, aware that the Social Contract had created labour hostility that could jeopardise other investment projects in the motor industry, the Prime Minister James Callaghan felt inclined to add his encouragement and to say, 'Ford has shown confidence in Britain, in return we must do all we can to justify the confidence by maintaining high productivity and reliability and good industrial relations.'[5]

The cutbacks in public spending required by the IMF in 1976 did not affect the government's financial arrangements with BL and Chrysler. Since part of the government's overall intention in 1976 was to direct more resources into productive investment and away from the social services, so the Ryder and the Lever plans escaped the axe.

Effects on Conduct

Although the government entered this period with a prices commission, in May 1976 price controls on cars were relaxed in order to encourage investment.[6] Consequently the car manufacturers were more free to set prices. In setting prices for exports one aspect of regulatory policy in 1976 necessitated higher export prices.[7] In order to increase taxes to meet its IMF agreement the government placed politics before economics. Instead of raising VAT, which would have been politically unpopular, they increased the employer's national insurance contribution by two per cent. This, to the majority of the population, did not look like a tax increase; though ultimately the consumer paid it. However, since this tax on employers could not be taken off exports nor imposed on imports, as VAT could, it meant an unfavourable relative change in British prices, both at home and overseas. British exports were rendered more expensive and imports cheaper than would have been the case if VAT had been increased.

Effects on Performance

Generally the constraints imposed by the IMF combined with the shift
to monetarism meant less government use of fiscal policy, and so less
impact on the UK motor industry via this means than in earlier years.
In terms of influencing industry the government relied more upon a
policy of industrial strategy of 'picking winners'. This strategy is now
examined under competitions policy.

Competitions Policy

With the downplaying of demand management policy after 1975 the
government became more interested in supply-side economic policies
with a view to improving efficiency and encouraging growth in the
economy. It did this via industry strategies affecting specific industrial
sectors. This change of approach was reflected in the establishment of
the NEB, the setting up of NEDC sector working parties in 1975 and
the 1975 Industrial Strategy Act. For the UK motor industry it was
apparent in financial support for British Leyland and Chrysler (UK).
Industrial strategy, therefore, became the chief means through which
the government attempted to influence competitiveness in the UK
motor industry in the mid-1970s. But by 1978 the Labour government
had become disillusioned with these efforts to directly stimulate chosen
industrial sectors, a disillusionment shown in the government attitude
to the motor industry.[8]

Other developments in competitions policy in the late seventies
included a consolidating Act covering past restrictive trade practices
and resale prices legislation, and a Green Paper, *A Review of Monopolies
and Mergers Policy*.[9] Neither had noteworthy consequences for the UK
motor industry.

Once again competitions policy is examined under two headings. In
this chapter we examine first British Leyland and then the multinationals.

The NEB and British Leyland

As many critics at the time had anticipated, the overly optimistic goals
of the Ryder plan were not achieved. Between 1975 and 1979 BL's
market share declined from 32 per cent in 1975 to around twenty per
cent in 1979, whilst little improvement occurred in productivity due to
overmanning. This overmanning itself was partly the result of government
labour policy which made laying off workers difficult and expensive.
To a large extent the government had made a cross for its own back. By
becoming directly responsible for, and therefore more closely associated

with, BL in the public eye, any policy which had unfavourable effects on BL or employment or the balance of payments had obviously greater political ramifications than heretofore. Consequently, even though the Ryder goals were not met, it became extremely difficult, politically, to instigate the investment cutbacks Ryder had proposed when production targets were not met. Furthermore, abandonment of the Ryder plan was frustrated until 1977 by the fact that Ryder himself had been appointed head of the NEB, the government body with responsibility for vetoing funds for BL. Any NEB veto would implicitly have suggested that the original Ryder plan, and so Ryder himself, had been wrong.

Throughout 1976 BL failed to meet its objectives and in late 1976 the government's frustrations became clear. Mr Varley declared the government's financial commitment, 'is not of course open ended. The government will insist on positive progress from management, unions and all employees.'[10] In spring 1977 the NEB was reported to have considered closing BL.[11] The final straw had been a massive toolmakers strike, a consequence of Stage Two pay parity frustration, in March 1977. The Ryder plan itself was officially abandoned at this time when a freeze on capital spending at BL was imposed. Nevertheless, the grave consequences for the balance of payments and employment, if BL had been closed, as well as equity considerations about innocent parties who would have been made redundant or bankrupt, meant investment expenditures, including those for a new Mini, eventually got the go-ahead in the early summer.

The resignation of Ryder in July 1977 opened the door to changes at BL, which by that time had had £350 million of government money. Furthermore, over the summer of 1977 it became clear that the public had become disenchanted with government hand-outs to BL. The Prime Minister was reported by the *Daily Express* to have commented to his Ministers that, 'If we could get rid of the motor industry perhaps our image wouldn't be so bad.'[12] In addition, as North Sea oil began to flow, contributing fifteen billion pounds to the balance of payments 1976-8, concern over the pound became less. Thus, even though car import levels approached fifty per cent of the home market the pressing need for BL to produce import substitutes diminished.

Late in 1977 Mr Michael Edwardes of the NEB and Chloride company was loaned by Chloride for three years to head BL. The terms of his appointment showed that the government intended him to have more freedom of scope to reorganise BL, demonstrating both less government concern about political repercussions, an attitude made possible by reduced public concern over BL, and also the government's own growing disillusionment with its own interventionist industrial strategy.

The reorganisation of BL introduced by Mr Edwardes in 1978 reflected the rejection of the earlier industrial strategy and included the abandonment of physical targets such as had characterised the Ryder plan. In condemnation of the earlier methods, Mr Edwardes said, 'We have had enough of instant re-organisation.'[13] Instead, sectors at BL were given more autonomy and required to make profits. Between 1978 and 1980 £850 million was to be spent on a trimmed and shortened Ryder plan. Half of this money was to be provided by the government as equity capital, in order to facilitate borrowing by the company from outside sources. The NEB put up £250 million and the Ministry of Industry £200 million. Finally, BL was decentralised by removing the heads of each of the four sectors of the company, Cars, Truck and Bus, Special Products and Leyland International, from the company board.

Effects on Basic Conditions. The decision to provide investment funds to BL, despite failure to meet the Ryder goals, affected conditions of supply. It meant import substitutes would be produced and the attempt to curb imports would be continued even though North Sea oil revenues meant the balance of payments was less critical.

Events at BL in 1976 and 1977 had demonstrated a major flaw in the Ryder plan. Ryder had assumed that investment cutbacks and threats of cutbacks would encourage conformation by the labour force with the plan's goals. In practice in 1976 and 1977 investment cutbacks were difficult, if not impossible, to implement without damaging yet further prospects of achieving the Ryder plan goals. The use of such methods only created more labour confrontation and hostility, not conformation as had been intended originally.

Effects on Structure. It is likely that by 1978 BL, without government funding, would have gone into liquidation or been absorbed, in whole or in pieces, by foreign firms. If the Ryder plan had been followed to the letter it is likely that much, if not all, of BL would have folded in 1977 when labour troubles caused the company to fail hopelessly to meet its targets and to have its worst financial year since 1974, when financial problems had led BL to the government for assistance and the Ryder Report. Thus the structure of the UK motor industry was characterised in the late 1970s by one inefficient British company, BL, three multinational companies, all of which had become increasingly integrated with their European operations, and an ever increasing number of import offerings, notably from Europe and Japan but also from the

Comecon countries and, for 1979, South Korea (see Table 7.3). By allocating government funds to BL the British sector of the industry, albeit shrinking, was maintained.

Table 7.3: UK Market Shares, 1973 and 1978 (percentage)*

	1973	1978
BL	32	23
Ford	23	25
Peugeot Citroën Chrysler (UK)	12	11
GM	9	10
Datsun	4	6
Renault	4	4
Volkswagen	4	4
Fiat	3	5
Other	9	12

*In 1978 imports by Ford, Chrysler, GM and BL accounted for 13 per cent of total UK sales. In April 1979 they accounted for 20 per cent of UK sales, and over 50 per cent of Ford sales were imports.

Source: SMMT

Effects on Conduct. Government policy towards BL influenced product strategy, research and innovation, and pricing. First, the decision to go ahead with the new Mini for 1980 was made on non-commercial grounds. The small-car market was historically unprofitable (even the first Mini, whatever its innovative merits, had not made profits in its first decade of production) and by the late 1970s the small-car market was crowded with a number of excellent models. The go-ahead for a replacement was given so as to produce an import substitute. On purely commercial grounds the funds used for the new Mini would have likely produced a better return either outside the motor industry or in the production of a new mid-size Marina replacement. Secondly, by giving greater freedom of action to Edwardes in 1977 the opportunity for collaboration with other motor firms was expanded. It meant less concern for protecting jobs at BL. The first such collaboration was announced in 1979 when BL planned production of a Honda model in the mid-size car range.[14] This plan shortened the lead time and reduced the capital necessary for producing a much needed new model.

This seemed a sound strategy. In 1978 BL still produced 14 different outdated models at a time when European giants such as Ford and

Volkswagen each produced five.[15] New models were essential. In addition, reports that BL was short of design engineers implied that the advantage which it had had in the engineering field two decades earlier, when the Mini was introduced, had long dissipated.[16] Furthermore, with the interest on its loans running at £5 million per month, any opportunity to reduce capital expenditures on new models was attractive. In 1977 the company had even had to borrow to meet its wage bills.

The arms-length relationship given to Mr Edwardes, in the context of the public's general disgust with BL by late 1977, gave him more scope to cut investment plans. In September 1978 he threatened to cut, irrevocably, £32 million of investment at Bathgate unless a return to work took place. A worker there, reflecting his reaction based on earlier empty threats, commented, 'Michael Edwardes is talking through a hole in his head.'[17] The next day the cut was made and over 1,000 jobs permanently lost. In 1978 Edwardes also cut a £100 million plan to modernise BL's iron and light alloy foundries: in future BL would bring in more parts. Also, BL's second newest but too small plant at Speke, which had been plagued with labour problems since its creation by STI in 1960 as part of the government's regional policy, was closed. These cuts appeared to have some influence. When, in September 1978, Edwardes threatened to cut the whole volume car division of BL if a full strike was called, no strike took place; and so BL continued with its plan to remain in the volume car sector and to introduce new volume models.

The government's close involvement with BL also raised questions concerning business conduct and business ethics. In the summer of 1977 the *Daily Mail* ran a sensational exclusive story about BL paying bribes from a Ministry of Industry slush fund to get overseas orders and to help overseas agents avoid taxes.[18] Though the story was eventually shown to be what the Prime Minister called 'a display of political spite' and was based on forgeries, it raised important moral questions about firm conduct.[19] Bribery to get overseas orders was shown in the 1970s to be a fairly common form of international business by private corporations, but whether government-supported businesses could follow the same conduct was debatable.[20] Indeed, stricter ethical requirements at BL were demonstrated later in the year when BL's current chairman, Sir Richard Dobson, said at a private dinner that BL 'bribed wogs' and was forced to resign.[21]

Finally, the decision in early 1978 to provide additional government funds to BL enabled BL to introduce a short-term superdeal policy affecting market conduct. By offering cheap finance and high trade-in prices BL was able to effectively cut prices and so substantially increase its market share on a short-term basis.

Effects on Performance. In terms of the government's overall economic objectives, industrial policy in the post-Ryder-plan period had several consequences. As noted before, the investment funds allocated to BL could probably have been more efficiently used elsewhere. Indeed, the government's admonition to the NEB to expect a lower rate of return on funds given to BL reflected the fact that non-economic concerns influenced the government's industrial strategy for BL.[22]

Table 7.4: Return on Capital Employed, 1977

	Percentage
GM	34
Toyota	27
Ford	26
Nissan	20
Peugeot-Citroën	17
Volkswagen/Audi	16
Chrysler	5
Fiat	5
Renault	3
BL	1

Source: *Investors Chronicle*, 2 Feb. 1979.

Obviously the funds protected jobs, though by 1976 the CPRS had come to the conclusion that the closure of a BL plant would not have serious repercussions for employment in the components industry.[23] (In 1975 Chrysler (UK)'s bail-out had been justified, in part, by some hefty assumptions about employment losses in the components industry.) The decision to provide additional equity and loans to BL to keep the company viable had favourable effects on the balance of payments. In 1977 the motor industry was still the country's premier exporter of manufactured goods. Although the components industry had long since surpassed the car industry by value of exports (see Table 7.5), the argument that a sizeable home car industry was essential to the long-term viability of the components industry and its ability to contribute to the balance of payments held merit. Certainly the demands made on the components industry in the early 1960s by the UK motor industry, and the research and development these demands inspired, were partly responsible for the success of the components industry in the 1970s. Therefore, for the long term, subsidising the UK car industry held potential for greater contributions by the components industry to the balance of payments in the future. Lastly, the decision to continue to provide financial support to BL, despite the distressing performance in 1977, was partly based on equity grounds. It was argued that closing any car plant because performance objectives were not achieved, punished those who were responsible but also those who were not.

Table 7.5: Analysis of Motor Industry Exports as Percentage of UK Total Exports, 1952-77

Year	Motor industry as percentage of UK exports	Car industry as percentage of UK exports	Commercial vehicles as percentage of UK exports*	Components as percentage of UK exports**
1952	12.7	4.3	5.1	3.3
1953	11.7	4.1	4.2	3.4
1954	12.8	4.6	4.6	3.6
1955	13.4	4.5	4.8	4.1
1956	12.6	3.8	4.9	3.9
1957	13.5	4.8	4.8	3.9
1958	14.7	5.8	4.5	4.4
1959	15.9	6.5	4.8	4.6
1960	16.9	6.2	5.5	5.2
1961	15.1	3.9	5.9	5.3
1962	16.5	5.5	5.8	5.2
1963	16.7	5.6	5.9	5.2
1964	16.8	5.8	5.6	5.4
1965	16.6	5.3	5.4	5.9
1966	15.9	4.6	5.4	5.9
1967	14.6	4.2	4.6	5.8
1968	14.5	4.5	4.2	5.8
1969	15.3	4.9	4.7	5.7
1970	14.4	4.1	4.4	5.9
1971	14.8	4.0	4.6	6.2
1972	13.5	3.4	3.9	6.2
1973	12.6	3.0	3.7	5.9
1974	11.4	3.2	3.4	4.8
1975	13.1	2.4	4.5	5.2
1976	12.7	2.5	4.3	5.9
1977	11.4	2.3	4.1	6.0

* Includes commercial vehicles, industrial trucks, dumper parts and dumpers, trailers and caravans, agricultural tractors
**Includes parts and accessories including rubber tyres and tubes, marine and industrial engines up to 200 BHP

Source: SMMT data.

Multinational Developments

After 1975 two developments characterised the experience of the multinational firms. First, the government's financial agreement with Chrysler meant a special relationship existed between Chrysler and the government. Secondly, there was greater integration by the multinationals of their UK and other European operations.

One condition of the government's financial aid to Chrysler in 1975 was that a closer integration of Chrysler (UK) and Chrysler (France) should take place. The government was particularly concerned that Chrysler (UK) should not become just a back-up assembly plant for the larger French operations. Terms of their financial agreement with Chrysler included a requirement that all of certain components for all of Chrysler's European models be produced in the UK. This condition was taken by Ford and GM as an indication that the government would not look askance at greater European integration of their activities too. During the late 1970s this integration occurred.

The government's considerable financial aid to Chrysler (UK) enabled the company to claim in 1976 that it was viable. In July 1978 the government approved a new three-year plan with Chrysler (UK) which it was hoped would help stem the mounting tide of imports. Consequently the UK government was completely taken aback when a month later, in August 1978, Chrysler (US) announced it had agreed to sell Chrysler (UK) to Peugeot of France. The limited government involvement in this takeover after three years of close communication was reflected by Mr Varley's statement that the government was only informed of the development three days before the public announcement.[24] Confronted with a *fait accompli*, even though a government veto would have been possible, the government could do little more than insist on certain conditions and express indignation.

The sale of Chrysler (UK) and Chrysler (France) by Chrysler (US) to Peugeot-Citroën was part of a general retrenchment programme undertaken by Chrysler (US) in the late 1970s. By far the smallest of the 'big three' US multinational producers, Chrysler had made inadequate profits for several years both at home and overseas to enable it to finance necessary research and development. Drastic measures were required. Many overseas interests, therefore, were sold off, for instance its South African and Australian divisions, in an attempt to raise the nearly eight billion dollars Chrysler felt it needed over the next five years for new models.[25] The largest divestiture was that of its European operations to Peugeot.

Peugeot-Citroën took over £400 million of Chrysler's debt and gave Chrysler (US) £230 million and fifteen per cent of Peugeot-Citroën stock in return for Chrysler (UK) and Chrysler (France). As a result Peugeot-Citroën-Chrysler could claim 18 per cent of the European market, had total sales of over two million and was larger than VW, Fiat or Renault.

Table 7.6: Share of World Production, by Company, 1978

	Percentage
GM	25.5
Ford	16.2
Peugeot-Citroën	7.3
VW/Audi	7.2
Toyota	6.9
Nissan	6.0
Renault	5.4
Chrysler	5.3
Fiat	4.4
BL	2.4
Honda	2.1
Toyo Goyo	1.8
Mitsubishi	1.8
Daimler-Benz	1.5
Seat	1.3
BMW	1.1

Source: *Investors Chronicle*, 2 Feb. 1979.

In 1975, under the Lever plan, the government had made a financial commitment to Chrysler of up to £162 million. Government approval of the Chrysler-Peugeot merger was necessary, but there was no choice. If the government had vetoed the deal, Chrysler would undoubtedly have closed down Linwood. With an election in the offing and the Scottish vote crucial to the Labour Party, there was no political alternative but to let the deal go through. In any case it made much sense. Chrysler (UK) was helping to bleed Chrysler (US) to death, whilst Peugeot's offer was not unattractive. Peugeot promised to continue with the Iran deal and to allow government representatives to sit on the board of Chrysler (UK). There would be no plant closures or redundancies. New models planned would not be cancelled. UK suppliers would be given access to the Peugeot group which had traditionally produced many of its own parts. Non-unionised Peugeot would recognise the trade unions and agreed to negotiate a pay settlement within the government's guidelines.[26]

On the supply side it has been shown how, at BL, government threats of investment cutbacks failed to convince the labour force either that the UK motor industry had a future or to conform to Ryder's goals. The Lever plan for Chrysler met with a similar fate. Throughout 1976 and 1977 there was a series of strikes that would have been suicidal had the labour force believed in the company's long-term future. Reflecting the labour force's lack of faith, 2,300 men applied for 1,300 voluntary redundancies in 1976 at Chrysler.[27]

Effects on Structure. The government's industrial strategy as regards the multinationals had important consequences for the industry's structure, for it effectively gave the go-ahead for a much closer integration with the European multinationals. By 1979 over half of the Ford cars sold in the UK were imports as was a large proportion of the cars sold by GM and Chrysler. Indeed, in 1979 Ford of Britain produced 400,000 fewer cars in the UK than it had in 1969 despite a larger share of the UK market. Increasingly, large amounts of the investment in the UK made by the multinationals was in the pre-assembly stages of production, for example Ford's major engine plant at Bridgend. This led to accusations by the unions that Ford and the other multinationals were disinvesting in Britain.[28] As regards assembly operations this made sense.[29] In 1977 the *Financial Times* reported that the multinationals no longer took the 'UK-view' with regard to their operations.[30] However, this reflected the would-be global trend of the whole world motor industry. All automobile producers throughout the world, as energy requirements, environmental requirements, development requirements and congestion requirements dictated smaller global cars for increasingly similar markets, tended to spread their operations. For example, despite high wage costs, considerable investment in Austria was made by the motor companies because the Austrians, without offsets, found the eight per cent of their balance of trade which went on cars and car-related products a particular handicap for economic management.[31] Without some form of offset they might well have had to introduce some form of import controls on cars. In the USA VW set up an assembly plant and the Japanese were reported to be looking for assembly sites there also.[32] Britain was a part of this general European and world integration by the multinationals. In the UK it had been encouraged and speeded up by the government's bail-out of Chrysler (UK) in 1975, had been approved by the CPRS in 1976, who concluded that with the integration of Chrysler (UK) and Chrysler (France) the UK car industry for the first time no longer had too many producers, and made sense in view of the increasing volumes at which economies of scale existed in the motor industry. Finally, since labour relations had traditionally been at their worst in the UK at the final assembly stage, it was inevitable that the multinationals would tend to shy away from investment there and towards components where labour relations and productivity were relatively better.

Effects on Conduct. The increased integration of the UK car industry with its European multinational counterparts had obvious consequences for firm conduct. Product strategy and research and innovation were increasingly based on the European or world view. For example, Ford assembled all Capri and Granada models in Germany and all Fiestas in Spain. Vauxhall and Opel designs became increasingly similar. Bucking the trend to less assembly in the UK, GM moved the production of its Cavalier model from Belgium to the UK in 1978. Despite government conditions on the Chrysler-Peugeot takeover, further integration and model standardisation were inevitable there too.

Effects on Performance. Following the conclusions of the 1976 CPRS study on the Chrysler (UK) bail-out, the move to greater integration of the multinationals was potentially favourable from the efficiency standpoint. Since World War II Vauxhall and Chrysler (UK) had been far too small to exploit economies of scale, so that European integration was beneficial. Furthermore, since the alternative to such integration for both companies would likely have been a total cessation of UK operations at some time in the 1980s, the development was favourable from the point of view of employment and the balance of payments.

Import and Export Policy

By 1976 imports were taking forty per cent of the UK home market and Mr Eric Varley, the Industry Minister, stated that such levels 'cannot be accepted'.[33] Clearly the policy goal of the government was to curb imports. In practice no policy tool to achieve this goal existed. The majority of imports came from the EEC countries and, following the 1974 referendum, Britain was fully committed to the community and its internal free trade policies. By 1975 the tariff on EEC cars was 4.4 per cent, versus ten per cent on imported cars from most other markets, notably Japan. Against Japan, the second largest importing group to the UK and taking about ten per cent of the home market in 1976, limited action could be taken.

The tools used to curb Japanese imports included pleas, threats and technical restrictions. In 1976 a delegation from the SMMT, along with the Minister of Industry, made the first of what became annual pilgrimages to Japan to negotiate voluntary import limits. However, the delegation was on weak ground. First, such requests were contrary to the spirit of GATT agreements. Secondly, the Japanese Automobile Manufacturing Association claimed that the UK had an overall trade surplus with Japan, and that demands for voluntary import quotas were groundless.[34] Thirdly, it was almost impossible for MITI to administer voluntary quotas, for although by 1976 such manufacturers as Nissan and Toyota were well established in the UK market, others such as Suzuki and Suburu had not yet attempted to enter the market and argued, reasonably enough, that they had a right as much as the major Japanese manufacturers to attempt to sell in the UK.[35] Finally, and as events proved, the Japanese argued that curbing Japanese imports to the UK only opened up the market immediately for more EEC and Comecon imports and, for the future, for South Korean imports. In spite of these arguments threats of quotas by the British obtained some agreement from the Japanese to limit imports to Britain between 1976 and 1979. Furthermore, by bringing attention to the Japanese use of 'technical restrictions' on imports to Japan and setting a goal, however unrealistic, of one UK export to Japan for every import from Japan by 1984, some help to the UK's slipping exports may have been obtained: in 1977 BL formed an agreement with Mitsui to sell 5,000 cars in Japan.[36] Indeed, the use of technical restrictions was not beyond the UK government. In 1976 Toyota was refused an Industrial Development Certificate to build an import centre at Bristol.[37]

Other efforts were made to limit imports. In 1977 the EEC accused Britain of using regulations in order to control imports. Under the 'Motor Vehicles (Type Approval) (Great Britain) Regulations, 1976', every imported model had to have governmental approval that it met legal requirements. This involved considerable bureaucracy and cost, since it meant every car imported after 1978 had to be granted an approval certificate. France and Italy protested that other EEC members only set standards for components. Then in 1978 British Leyland, with government financing, introduced the superdeal sales effort in which BL offered higher-than-market trade-in prices and lower-than-market credit terms on new car sales, effectively subsidising the sale of BL cars. BL's share of the market rose by nearly ten per cent.

As concern over import levels mounted and dominated the headlines, the fact that the motor industry was still Britain's largest exporter of manufactured goods was rather overshadowed. Still, the government continued in its efforts to increase car exports as well as curb imports. Iran was persuaded to increase purchases of the Chrysler Payakan (the old Hillman Hunter) from 70,000 in 1977 to 250,000 in 1980. In 1978 the NEB agreed to put forward the necessary investment funds for the new Mini, not because it looked like a good commercial venture in the crowded small-car market, but because it would provide overseas dealers with a complete range of models and so, it was hoped, help the sales of larger British models. Also, at home, it would act as an import substitute.

The stipulation in the Chrysler (UK) financial aid programme that Chrysler (UK) must not become just a back-up assembly plant to Chrysler (France) but must be integrated and produce all of some components affected import and export levels. Ford and General Motors took this directive to Chrysler to sanction their own further integration of European operations with considerable consequences for the structure of the UK motor industry, as discussed under competitions policy.

Increased integration by the multinationals meant that the area of common interest with BL was reduced. This limited the government's scope in policy-making for imports and exports. In 1976 BL asked for taxes on imports. They also asked for quotas on imports. Understandably neither Ford nor GM agreed to these proposals.[38]

Effects on Basic Conditions

Since 1945 the concept of two markets, a largely captive home market based on protection and the desire of some consumers to buy British, and a more competitive overseas market, had existed. After 1970 lower tariffs and EEC membership had reduced protection and made the home market less captive. After 1975 this trend continued as the patriotic consumer found it harder to buy British. As the multinationals' European operations became increasingly integrated it became difficult to identify which were truly British cars. Traditionally British cars, for instance Ford Cortinas, were sourced from Germany, Spanish-assembled Ford Fiestas had British power trains in them, some Vauxhall cars came from Germany and Belgium. Even BL on occasion shipped in Belgian-assembled Minis. Consequently, however much the consumer may have wanted to buy British, it became increasingly difficult for him to know if he really was.

The policies outlined above attempted to increase demand for UK cars at home and abroad and to limit the supply of foreign cars in the UK market. Their success was limited. In 1978 Mr Dell, the British Trade Secretary, expressed anger that the Japanese had exceeded their 1977 voluntary quotas.[39] They argued that a confusion existed between sales quotas and import quotas. In 1977 more-than-usual labour troubles in the UK industry meant inadequate supplies of British cars, so that as Japanese imports were restrained, EEC imports and Comecon imports filled the gap. This particularly angered Nissan and Toyota dealers, many of whom had invested large amounts on retail outlets and felt, reasonably enough, that they were being punished for being too successful.[40] Superdeal dramatically improved BL's market share, but only temporarily held off the imports. With the overthrow of the Shah in 1979 the Payakan exports, which had been passed on to Peugeot as part of the Chrysler sale, were placed in jeopardy as Iran's economy contracted and anti-occidental attitudes took hold. The failure of government policy to effectively restrain the growth of car imports was reflected by the fact that by 1979 imports held nearly sixty per cent of the UK market.

Nevertheless, the noise and concern expressed by the government over import levels was successful indirectly. In 1978 the *Financial Times* reported that foreign firms were deliberately buying components from Britain.[41] They did this partly because British components were competitive, but also as a defensive policy to placate the British government's concern over the effect of rising imports on the balance of trade, and therefore as a form of insurance against possible import quotas. Also it is highly possible that without the government's threats and expressions of concern Japanese imports would have risen more rapidly. Failure to adhere to the quotas did not imply that some restraint was not being exercised.

Effects on Structure

Failure to contain imports led to changes in the structure of the UK motor industry. As has been noted, foreign manufacturers, for mixed motives, bought British components, so that by the late 1970s the components industry was bigger in terms of employment, capital, sales and exports than the car industry.

As regards the car industry, by the late 1970s the market share of the major importers such as Nissan, VW, Renault, Fiat, Opel and Ford were comparable to those of Ford (UK), Chrysler (UK) and Vauxhall (see Table 7.3). At the same time, as BL's home market share slipped below twenty per cent, BL could no longer claim to be in the same world league as a volume producer as, for instance, Ford (see Table 7.6). In other words, by 1979 Ford (UK), Vauxhall and Chrysler (UK) had all become very much integrated into the European motor industry — a development encouraged by the Chrysler (UK) bail-out — whilst BL had become a secondary junior league producer.

Effects on Conduct

All the manufacturers, even BL, responded to the government's approval of international integration. Increasing numbers of Ford and Opel products were imported from Germany. At the same time more of Ford's investment in the UK went into the components field: the largest Ford investment in the UK in the late 1970s was £180 million for an engine plant at Bridgend in Wales. This factory will have a capacity to produce over 500,000 engines annually, more than Ford's total UK car production. It would seem that the better labour relations record in the components area, as opposed to assembly, explained Ford's product policy approach, for in 1978 Ford produced 250,000 fewer cars in the UK than it had in 1969, its increase in UK sales being derived from imports. Early in 1979 over half the Ford cars sold in the UK were imports, and about one third of both Vauxhall's and Chrysler's. Similarly, in 1976 BL began to expand its Belgian operations so as to be able to produce 150,000 cars there, and in 1978 three per cent of BL cars sold in the UK were imports. Government policy had therefore given an impetus to the UK car firms to do less final assembly in Britain.

By 1979 the concept of the global or world car had arrived. The energy crisis of the decade meant that around the world car demand had become increasingly homogeneous. Even in the United States smaller cars were in vogue. The global car was equally suitable for Britain so that specific British designs were no longer required and manufacturers produced basically the same models for all of Europe. The Ford Fiesta, the Chrysler Horizon, the VW Golf and the GM Chevette were typical examples. This global car development, added to the failure of the government to curb imports into the UK, affected model development at BL. There it was decided to go ahead and build the new Mini before building a larger model to replace the outdated Maxi/Allegro models. This was despite the fact that BL dealers wanted the mid-size model more and that it looked as though such a model would have made a bigger contribution to profits since the old Mini still sold well. High import levels explain why the Mini came first. In the UK, when the decision was made, British Ford Cortinas and Escorts dominated mid-size and fleet car sales, whilst most of the smaller car rivals to BL were foreign. Consequently the government, through the NEB, favoured production of an import substitute, the new Mini, even if it was commercially less attractive. A brand loyalty theory also favoured NEB support for the development of a new Mini. This theory argues, first, that people tend to buy the same brand and, secondly, that people's first new car is a small one. Therefore, it was concluded, BL needed a small car at home and overseas to bait consumers for larger model purchases at a later date.

Effects on Performance

By giving more encouragement to imports, via the Chrysler integration policy, than discouragement, via voluntary import quotas, it would appear that the balance of payments and full employment goals in particular suffered. Table 6.5 shows the dramatic change in the UK balance of trade in cars. However, this disappointing trend was to some extent mitigated by the favourable growth of the components industry (see Table 7.5). In some ways the components industry benefited from the rise in imports. As noted above, Ford favoured Wales for the production of engines whilst considerable European and Japanese purchases of UK components were made as voluntary offsets for car imports. Nevertheless, at the same time more components were imported into Britain, not just as part of increasing international integration but also as replacement parts on earlier vehicle imports. Therefore, despite the components sector's growth it is hard to avoid the conclusion that failure to curb car imports meant fewer jobs overall and a worsened balance of payments.

The long-term balance of payments and full employment goals were particularly vulnerable as European integration took place. The UK components industry's success in the 1970s was partly a result of two historical factors. First, the lack of vertical integration in the UK motor industry had meant large components suppliers such as GKN and Lucas had always existed in Britain. In the 1970s these large firms were in a good position to exploit the economies of scale which had developed in the components industry. Secondly, early development of front-wheel drive cars by BMC in the 1960s had given these large suppliers a technical lead in this area. As the US, Japanese and Europeans all turned to front-wheel drive designs the UK components manufacturers benefited. Consequently the competitive position of the UK components industry in the 1970s can be seen as the result of a reasonably strong, technically advanced car industry in the early 1960s. For the longer-term future, therefore, the UK components industry, without a similar strong UK car assembly industry as a base to make technical and volume demands on it, was in a precarious position as regards its ability to make contributions to the UK's economic growth, full employment and balance of payments in the long run. And with the increasing use of plastics, advanced electronics and other sophisticated technology to meet the 1970s and 1980s energy problems, rapid change in this sector of the motor industry was to be anticipated.

Taxation Policy

The use of taxation to manipulate the demand for cars, as well as for generating revenue (see Table 6.8), continued into the late 1970s, though in rather different circumstances. In the 1940s tax changes had been introduced to encourage exports.[42] In the 1970s taxation policy was used to discourage imports. For example, in 1976 plans were introduced to make the benefits of the private use of company cars with engines greater than 1800cc subject to income tax. The 1800cc limit was chosen because many of the up-market German cars, such as BMWs which were popular as fringe benefits, had engines larger than 1800cc.[43] Also in 1976 the government abandoned proposed plans to abolish the flat rate licence tax and put an additional tax on petrol of 16-17 pence to compensate for the lost revenue.[44] This was because higher petrol prices would have encouraged more small-car sales, a sector of the car market in which the UK car industry had become particularly uncompetitive. In the 1977 budget, in order to increase government revenues, car licences were increased and it was proposed to increase the tax on petrol by five pence. However, the minority Labour government could only get support from the Liberal Party for its Finance Bill if it rescinded the increase in petrol tax, and this it did. In June 1979 VAT on all goods and services including cars was increased to fifteen per cent to compensate for revenues lost to the government through cuts in direct taxes made to stimulate the economy.

Consequences of Taxation Policy

By the late 1970s imports had taken approximately fifty per cent of the UK market and an even greater proportion of the market of private buyers (as opposed to large companies which still tended to buy British). Consequently the taxation changes outlined above which tended to discourage small-car purchases had only limited scope as protective devices against imports in the aggregate. Whilst British cars may have been slightly more competitive in the middle-size range, imports were popular in both categories. However, maintaining the flat rate licence fee and keeping petrol prices in Britain amongst the lowest in Europe encouraged the use of uneconomical engines and possibly some waste of North Sea oil. The switch to higher VAT was offset by lower direct taxes and probably had little effect on demand.

Finally, one inconsequential but interesting outcome of British taxation laws concerned BL. In 1977 BL wanted to re-hire its former production manager, Mr G. Turnbull, who had been working for the Korean Hyunda car company. Britain's highly progressive personal tax system made a mutually satisfactory remuneration for Mr Turnbull and the government impossible. So, to circumvent their own tax laws, the government hired Mr Turnbull as a European-based consultant.[45]

Labour Policy

Officially the major development in government policy and labour relations between 1975 and 1979 was the Bullock Report published in January 1977.[46] However, its proposals for worker directors and greater worker participation were unacceptable to labour and management, the report was shelved and therefore had little consequence for the motor industry. Similar recommendations for greater worker participation had been rejected at BL in 1971 and, as part of the Ryder proposals, in 1975. For the industry the implementation of the Social Contract, its implications on pay parities and the use of the motor industry as a testing ground for the pay policy had considerable repercussions.

Previous chapters noted how, by the 1970s, worker solidarity in the motor industry had been reduced and replaced by a certain amount of worker rivalry. Stages One and Two of the Social Contract exacerbated this trend, first, by offering a £6 flat rate pay increase across the board for 1975/6 and, secondly, by successfully achieving a fall in real wages between 1975 and 1977. A massive strike at BL in March 1977 by the usually conservative toolmakers over the reduced pay parities resulting from the Social Contract reflected the frustration Stages One and Two had caused most dramatically. Although strikes over pay differentials had plagued the industry in 1976, the toolmakers' strike in early 1977 which lasted a month, idled over 20,000 workers and cost BL £150 million, was the largest pay differential strike. The strike was the largest of over 700 at BL that year, a sizeable proportion of which reflected frustrations over pay and pay differentials. The strike also put the final nail in the coffin of the Ryder plan which had relied so heavily on improved labour relations.

Traditionally Ford had been the testing ground in the private sector for government income policies. In 1969, 1971 and 1974 it had been so used, and in 1977 and 1978 it was so used again. Scared of jeopardising the Bridgend engine plant, union leaders persuaded Ford workers in October 1977 to settle for twelve per cent and fringe benefits for the following twelve months: this just exceeded the government's Stage Three ten per cent guidelines. However, in October 1978, having seen their relative earnings decline over the previous year, the Ford workers were less compliant, and a huge strike took place against the government's pay policy.

Whilst no courts of inquiry were established and whilst the Bullock Report was shelved, the government, through the effects of its pay policy on labour relations, exerted considerable influence on the basic conditions, structure, conduct and performance of the UK car industry.

Effects on Basic Conditions

Constant strikes and disruptions in the components and car industry over government pay policy affected car demand. Unable to obtain British cars for immediate delivery, yet more consumers turned to foreign cars. This was particularly so in 1977. In February BL was closed down by their toolmakers strike. In August Lucas toolmakers closed the whole industry. When in 1978 British cars were more easily available the demand was no longer there for them. For British Leyland this meant that market shares fell from over thirty per cent in 1975 to around twenty per cent in 1979. For the multinationals it encouraged greater sourcing of completed cars, and to some extent components, from European plants. Whilst these trends were likely in any case, pay-policy-incited labour stoppages encouraged them further.

The pay policy also encouraged some interesting alliances and hostilities within the industry's labour force. One example was the 1978 strike at Ford against the suggested five per cent Stage Four ceiling. Ford management was clearly unprepared to fight inflation for the government. Rather than face a prolonged strike from a hostile labour force, Ford, after a four-week strike, said it would negotiate a pay settlement greater than the guideline. Sir Terence Becket, Ford (UK) chairman, justified the action saying,

> In discussions with the government and trade unions . . . the company has repeatedly and unsuccessfully sought to find a way through two diametrically opposed views. Ford shares the Government's concern about the control of inflation, to which the voluntary incomes policy is directed. It must, however, also be concerned about being able to manage in the proper interests of the business in both domestic and export markets — and many other companies whose livelihood depends upon it.[47]

Angered by this labour-management alliance to reject Stage Four the government imposed sanctions on Ford and cancelled government orders for 25,000 Ford vehicles worth nearly two hundred million pounds.[48] Another example of unusual alliances was the 1977 BL toolroom workers strike. Pay differential strikes inevitably involve higher-paid workers against lower-paid workers. At BL the high-paid toolroom workers and their shop stewards found themselves in opposition to moderate trade union leaders who were in support of the government's pay policy. In this case management sympathised with the toolroom workers. BL management fruitlessly requested the government to allow pay increases beyond the Social Contract so long as the total wage bill of the company did not exceed the ceilings. At BL conflicting labour interests also developed when it was decided to close the Speke plant which had a terrible history of labour strife and poor quality production. Although two thousand workers at Speke would be made redundant, transfer of production to Cranley reduced the likelihood of redundancies there. In general the other BL workers showed little enthusiasm for a strike to support the notoriously troublesome Speke workers.[49] In June 1978 all one thousand foremen at Ford went on strike. Their reason was violence against them from the workforce.[50] As visible lower management they caught the full fury of labour hostility in the car factories. But, whatever the hostilities and alliances involved, the increased labour strife caused by the Social Contract contributed to the failure to improve productivity in the industry between 1975 and 1979, and the failure to supply British cars even when the demand for them existed.

One favourable outcome of the Social Contract, which required that pay settlements be for one year, was the encouragement it gave to the implementation of a rational pay structure at BL. Between 1975 and 1979 some order was injected into BL's 'crazy-paving' envy-provoking wage settlement system. It enabled BL, by being allowed a once-only exception to the one settlement per year rule, to set up arrangements for a company-wide settlement for November 1979.[51]

Effects on Structure

Poor labour relations, particularly in assembly, served to discourage final assembly operations in Britain despite relatively low wage rates (see Table 7.2). This was reflected in Ford's reduction of final assembly in the UK over the decade, and that even BL expanded some of its final assembly to Belgium at a time when it was closing plants, notably Speke, in Britain. As already noted, these developments would likely have occurred in any case, but labour problems aggravated by the Social Contract gave added impetus.

Effects on Conduct

Poor labour relations affected investment decisions by the multinationals and BL. In the case of the multinationals poor labour relations meant new investment and new models would be made elsewhere. The trade unions claimed there was a disinvestment in the UK motor industry in the late 1970s, although it is impossible to know to what extent a reduction in final assembly operations was offset by increased production of in-house components. Still, as a percentage of UK sales, Ford (UK) investment between 1971 and 1974 fell from eight per cent to four per cent, whilst planned investment from 1976 to 1982 was a 'mere' one billion pounds, even less than BL planned to spend. BL's capability to switch model production to other countries was limited. Nevertheless, BL did close Speke, because of poor labour relations, and transferred production of the TR7 to Cranley. Following a series of strikes in 1976 BL froze investment plans. A £22 million investment at Bathgate was also cancelled because of labour problems in 1978. However, the main consequence of labour problems at BL was the delay of investment. For instance, the colossal 1977 toolmakers strike led to threats of cancelling the new Mini and the closure of Longbridge. In the end the NEB and BL lacked the resolve to carry through such threats. Instead investment was merely postponed. Of course such delays were inimical to BL's becoming competitive once again; time and tide waiting neither for man nor lame duck industries.

Effects on Performance

The Social Contract had mixed effects on the achievement of the country's overall economic goals. Its success from 1975 to 1978 in slowing down inflation and helping to strengthen the pound is difficult to assess. Healey's strict monetarist policies, government expenditure cutbacks and the considerable revenues from North Sea oil after 1976, all contributed to Britain's improved economic performance between 1975 and 1979. In terms of the motor industry's ability to contribute to the country's overall economic goals, the Social Contract had negative consequences. The labour frustration it caused led to inefficiency and waste, both through lost production during strikes and poor morale on the shop floor. In the short term the balance of payments suffered because imports filled the vacuum created when British cars, because of strikes, were unavailable to those who still wanted them. For the longer term the balance of payments, economic growth and full employment all suffered when decisions to invest outside of Britain were made or when decisions to invest in Britain were delayed. If the alternative to the Social Contract really was hyperinflation, the price was worth paying. If, as many economists believe, government cutbacks and strict monetary policy were the main reasons for the fall in the inflation rate, not the Social Contract, then the labour frustrations caused by the Social Contract proved expensive and ran counter to achieving the country's overall economic goals.[52]

Transport Policy

Despite the decline of the British motor industry in the 1970s, the government's commitment to the private car did not waver. The 1977 White Paper on Transport reflected this.[53] The paper supported the use of cars, wanted more subsidies for buses, and advocated that more rural railways be eliminated. Still, this commitment did not prevent the government from cutting road expenditures by £80 million in 1976 as part of its £730 million cuts in public expenditures. In 1977 the government examined the question of whether lorries paid their fair share of transport costs, and in 1978 began a programme to pave over some railways so that they could be used for commuter transport.

Environmental Policy

Never as enthusiastic about environmental policy as regards the car as the Americans, and even less inclined towards it following the post-OPEC slow growth years, little influence was exerted by the government in this sphere. Financial support for the new BL Mini might be interpreted as an energy conservation measure, but the Mini was more important as an import substitute. Following the petrol shortage in the summer of 1979, the government limited its involvement to providing petrol-saving driving tips. In 1977 a grant for £400,000 was given to the Greater London Council to experiment with electric vehicles, and other grants amounting to over £2 million were made to examine alternatives to the internal combustion engine.[54] Therefore, between 1975 and 1979 environmental policies took a back seat to efforts to control inflation in general and to maintain a viable British sector of the motor industry in particular.

Regional Policy

Though regional policy had had its heyday in the late 1950s and early 1960s for the motor industry, it continued to be used. Areas of high unemployment still offered special investment grants. In the late 1970s one development of interest was the establishment of a new car factory in West Belfast, Northern Ireland, to build a new car.[55] The new car, a luxury high-speed sports model, was the inspiration of an ex-GM (US) executive. The car, called the Delorean after its creator, would create two thousand jobs in an area where the unemployment rate was thirty per cent. The Delorean car factory was estimated in 1978 to cost eighty million pounds. Delorean put up one quarter of this, the Ulster Department one half and the Northern Ireland Development Agency the rest.

Thus each job in this risky venture cost the government thirty thousand pounds. At the time of writing the car has not gone into production. Subsidies were also made to GM to build a new plant in Belfast which created six hundred new jobs at a cost of twelve thousand pounds each to the government.[56]

Summary

In the later 1970s the government made a number of efforts to revitalise the UK motor industry. Public funds were used to help BL and Chrysler (UK) make a comeback. Efforts were made to curb imports, both directly by extracting voluntary import quotas from the Japanese and through the use of technical restrictions to impede European imports, and indirectly by financing import substitutes and by holding down the price of petrol. For the most part the government ceased to use the industry as a tool to manage the economy.

These efforts had limited success. Other government policies, particularly the Social Contract, aggravated labour relations, the key element in a recovery by the industry. Labour relations were also harmed by the way in which the Ryder plan and the Lever plan sought to use threats of investment cutbacks as sticks to achieve their goals. Furthermore, the Lever plan for Chrylser's financial aid, by seeking greater integration of Chrysler (France) with Chrysler (UK), encouraged the other multinationals to move more car assembly operations overseas and to more fully integrate their UK operations with their operations around the globe: by 1979, in consequence, Ford was the leading car importer into Britain. In 1978 Chrysler (UK), with neither government intervention nor opposition, became part of the Peugeot group. By 1979, as a result of international integration in the world motor industry, it was hard to know how much of any car was British, German, Spanish, American or whatever. A further outcome of increased international integration and lower tariffs by 1979 was that the government's ability to determine how the UK motor industry performed had been considerably circumscribed. Still, the government continued to have a strong interest in the UK motor industry and remained totally committed to the car as the prime means of private transportation.

Notes

1. *Bank of England Quarterly Bulletin* (Mar. 1978), pp. 33-4.
2. *The Economist*, 18 Dec. 1976, p. 8.

3. *Financial Times*, 9 Aug. 1976.
4. *Business Week*, 30 Oct. 1978, p. 52.
5. *The Economist*, 17 Sept. 1977, p. 123.
6. *The Times*, 20 May 1976.
7. *The Economist*, 17 July 1976, p. 17.
8. *Financial Times*, 2 Feb. 1978.
9. Command 7198.
10. *The Economist*, 12 Feb. 1977, p. 107.
11. Ibid., 26 Feb. 1977, p. 101.
12. *Daily Express*, 9 Oct. 1978.
13. *The Economist*, 4 Feb. 1978, p. 108.
14. *Daily Telegraph*, 8 Apr. 1979.
15. *The Economist*, 14 Jan. 1978, p. 87.
16. Ibid.
17. Ibid., 23 Sept. 1978, p. 119.
18. *Daily Mail*.
19. *The Economist*, 28 May 1977, p. 21.
20. The most notorious case was the payment to Prince Bernhard of the Netherlands of large sums by the Lockheed Corporation.
21. *The Times*, 27 Oct. 1977.
22. *The Economist*, 8 Apr. 1978, p. 106.
23. *Financial Times*, 8 Apr. 1976.
24. *Daily Telegraph*, 6 July 1978.
25. *Business Week*, 15 May 1978, p. 23.
26. *Financial Times*, 29 Sept. 1978.
27. *The Economist*, 7 Feb. 1976, p. 75.
28. *The Economist*, 29 Apr. 1978, p. 124.
29. D.T. Jones and S.J. Prais, 'Plant Size and Productivity in the Motor Industry: Some International Comparisons', *Oxford Bulletin of Economics and Statistics*, vol. 40 (May 1978), pp. 131-51, discuss this in some detail.
30. *Financial Times*.
31. *The Economist*, 1 July 1978, p. 91.
32. *The Times*, 27 Oct. 1976.
33. Ibid., 20 Oct. 1976.
34. *The Economist*, 4 Feb. 1978, p. 108.
35. *Financial Times*, 4 Aug. 1977.
36. *The Economist*, 4 Mar. 1978, p. 95.
37. Ibid., 28 Aug. 1976, p. 68.
38. *Daily Mail*, 9 June 1976.
39. *Guardian*, 1 Mar. 1978.
40. *The Times*, 21 Sept. 1977.
41. *Financial Times*, 3 Feb. 1978.
42. See Chapter 3, p. 148.
43. *The Economist*, 12 June 1976, p. 61.
44. Ibid., 3 July 1976, p. 95.
45. Ibid., 16 July 1977, p. 91.
46. Parliament (Commons), *The Bullock Report: The Report of the Committee of Inquiry into Industrial Democracy* (HMSO, London, 1977).
47. *The Times*, 10 Oct. 1978.
48. *Financial Times*, 28 Sept. 1978.
49. *The Economist*, 22 Apr. 1978, p. 120.
50. Ibid., 10 June 1978, p. 120.
51. Ibid., 22 Oct. 1977, p. 89.
52. S. Brittan, 'The Futility of British Incomes Policy', *Challenge*, vol. 22

(May/June 1979), p. 5.
    53. *Transport Policy* (HMSO, London, 1977).
    54. *Scotsman*, 25 July 1978.
    55. *The Times*, 4 Aug. 1978.
    56. *Financial Times*, 2 Aug. 1978.

8 CONCLUSION

In this book I have attempted to analyse how government policies affected the UK motor industry between 1945 and 1979. I have shown that government policy did have a considerable influence on the UK motor industry. Sad to conclude, much of that influence was unintended and undesirable. From the introduction of export quotas in 1946 to the end of the Social Contract in 1979 a series of policies, many unfavourable as regards the motor industry, have been traced. And whilst, as regards the country's overall objectives, some of these policies had favourable outcomes, all too often the benefits were transitory or, even worse, negligible, when compared to the short-term and long-run costs imposed.

Some examples illustrate these points. Perhaps 'stop-go' demand management policies are the best known. In the short run stop-go forced an improvement in the balance of payments and, for the UK motor industry, squeezed more cars into exports. But stop-go also reduced industry profits, discouraged investment, worsened labour relations, emphasised the short-run basis of exports and, for the long run, weakened the motor industry and made it less competitive internationally. Another familiar example was regional policy, introduced in 1959. By forcing a geographical dispersion of an already too fragmented industry, efficiency and international competitiveness suffered. In addition, an unsuitable and fractious labour cohort was introduced into the car industry. But there were many other examples. Failure to enter the EEC until too late and failure to recognise the inevitability of the private car until very late affected efficiency and product designs in the car industry. Failure to reform labour relations successfully (instead reform aggravated labour relations) had negative consequences. The examples of unfortunate government policies are many.

In 1978 the NIESR said, 'Those who have searched for the causes of the British [motor] industry's failure have produced long lists of what is wrong', but goes on to say, 'if one is to pick on a single element as requiring resolution as a pre-condition to anything further . . . [we] side with those who emphasise the unsatisfactory state of labour relations'.[1] The conclusions of this book concur with the NIESR: labour relations in the UK motor industry in the late 1970s were highly unsatisfactory. But the historical approach of the book enables us to go

Table 8.1: UK Motor Vehicle Production as Share of Europe* and Japan

Year	Percentage
1963	26.9
1965	21.4
1967	17.4
1969	14.2
1971	12.1
1973	10.7
1975	7.8
1977	7.2

*France, Italy, Netherlands, Spain, Sweden, United Kingdom, West Germany

Sources: Central Policy Review Staff, *The Future of the British Car Industry* (HMSO, London, 1975), p. 60; SMMT data.

one step further and examine what went wrong in the past, and specifically what went wrong with labour relations. We have shown that in explaining bad labour relations there were many factors, some economic, others sociological, psychological and political. For example, the book notes one important sociological factor common to the labour force of the other major car-producing countries but not the UK: all other countries had access to a labour pool attempting to escape from immediate poverty and therefore more tolerant of the monotony of the car factories. Others have suggested that in Europe high absenteeism (Sweden) and high labour turnover (West Germany) were manifestations of the same frustrations which in the UK led to more costly labour militancy. But also important in the UK was how government policies aimed at increasing exports, regional balance, labour reform, incomes control and so on, all contributed to poor labour relations. Similarly if one looks for the causes of poor product ranges, dated designs, obsolete capital, unsatisfactory management and all the other problems of the industry, government policy is frequently a factor at some time in the past and frequently, as with labour relations, an important factor.

One conclusion of the book, therefore, is that government policies can have far-reaching consequences impossible to predict. This seems to fit the spirit of the times. In 1978 Denis Healey said it was time for private entrepreneurs to choose the winners in industry, reflecting his own party's disillusionment with government intervention.[2] In 1979 a Conservative government was elected with Margaret Thatcher as Prime Minister with a platform to reduce government interference and to follow generally more libertarian economic policies. The Conservative spokesman on economics, Nigel Lawson, said, 'We do not believe the government has a direct role to play in industry.'[3] The analysis of this book supports this prevalent mood that government planning is a much more complicated task than was thought in its heyday in the sixties. Planning can work. Planning can be useful. But perhaps, too, plans are best presumed to be undesirable unless they can be proved otherwise. Even the more modest industrial strategies of the seventies proved themselves difficult to implement and often costly in terms of foregone alternatives. BL is a prime example of this. Not only was the Ryder plan hopelessly wrong, but it is hard to believe the over one billion pounds it cost could not have been better spent either at Ford or in other industries than the motor industry.

One of the reasons that planning, whether of an industry or the economy, is so difficult is that assumptions about the future underlie plans. And whether it be the twenty-five per cent growth in gross national product which underlay *The National Plan*, or the likely no change in oil prices until 1980 forecast in 1975 by the CPRS, or the improvement in BL's market share by Ryder, such assumptions are often wrong. The difficulties of forecasting received much attention from the 1978 House of Commons Expenditure Report which devoted considerable space to the theme.

Another conclusion that this study of the UK motor industry leads to is that without industry concensus on a government policy, success is unlikely. Almost whenever the government forced a policy upon the industry against its will, the outcome was dire. Stop-go, the export quotas, labour reform attempts in 1968 and 1971, incomes policies and regional policy all illustrated the point. In all cases fewer overall benefits for the economy than anticipated by the government were generated whilst costs imposed on the industry exceeded expectations. The government tended to overestimate industry participation in its policies. All too often the industry proved a reluctant partner.

A further conclusion to be drawn from this study is that although government contributed to the decline of the UK motor industry, in the long run such a decline was likely in any case. A brief overview of possible future developments in the world motor industry discusses this.

Future Developments

Future development in the motor industry, both in the UK and Europe and the rest of the world, is likely to be exciting. Not only will energy requirements make great demands for change in the industry, but intense competition is likely to lead to more concentration and co-operative ventures worldwide. By 1979 the European and American markets had matured. With a car for every three people in Europe and every two in America, most demand in the future will be replacement demand. The areas of greater potential growth, Latin America, Asia and Africa are likely to be hard fought over by local producers as well as the Europeans and multinationals.

Table 8.2: World Car Sales Forecasts (millions of units)

	1976	1983	1990
North America*	11.4	14.2	15.6
Europe	9.1	11.4	14.0
Latin America	1.4	2.2	3.5
Africa	1.2	2.3	4.0
Asia	3.4	5.5	7.4
Total	26.5	35.6	44.4

*Includes Mexico

Source: *Business Week*, 10 Nov. 1978, p. 103.

Already in the United States the huge Chrysler corporation has found itself too small to compete successfully with GM and Ford. Even Ford, one of the largest corporations of any sort in the world, is strapped for adequate development funds. GM spent 2.7 billion dollars just to develop their 1980 X-car.[4] Development costs such as these (the US motor industry plans to spend seventy billion dollars just on retooling for new models between 1979 and 1985) augur poorly for many European producers who find it difficult to match such investment.[5] For example, Renault made a profit of only 2.6 million dollars in 1977 whilst planning seven billion dollars of investment between 1978 and 1982.[6] Many of the smaller European producers, such as Alfa Romeo and BL, are sustained only by government subsidies, and by comparison with planned American motor industry investments UK government aid to BL is trivial. Economies of scale in the motor industry are vast, competition intense, development funds formidable.

In the early eighties the European motor industry exhibits many of the characteristics of the UK motor industry in the early sixties, only on a larger scale. There are too many producers producing too many models with too much capacity. Rationalisation is essential but, in a relatively slow growth market (see Table 8.1), will prove difficult to achieve. If the past history of the UK motor industry is anything to go by, firms will attempt to remain as independents until brought to their knees. Then defensive mergers such as that between BMH and Leyland come about, but are likely to be thwarted in successful integration by the very slow growth markets that initiated them. In slow growth situations such mergers are often characterised by labour inefficiency, overmanning and management slack. In the sixties Japan showed that successful integration in the motor industry is easier when there is fast market growth, because it enables improved efficiency to take place without redundancies and lay-offs.

Still, a strong incentive to greater co-operation, if not mergers, already exists in Europe. American global cars and Japanese and South Korean products are likely to be increasingly apparent in the European and European-served markets in the 1980s. So far a number of co-operative ventures or alliances have taken place: Renault and AMC (sales); BL and Honda (a common model); Fiat and Peugeot (engine development); Chrysler and VW (engines); Volvo and Peugeot (engines); to name a few. Such trends seem likely to continue.

As Britain becomes more and more integrated into the European economy, her motor industry is likely to be increasingly a part of common ventures and alliances. The integration of Ford and GM's European operations was discussed in Chapter 7. Given Britain's relatively superior productivity in components, it is likely that Ford and GM will continue to do less assembly in the UK, although political considerations and the nature of current investments in the UK are likely to act as constraints on very rapid changes in this area. BL and Chrysler-Peugeot's future is more problematical. Michael Edwardes has given BL an eighty per cent chance of re-establishing itself as a volume car producer.[7] Even if government finances permit this, it is hard to believe that BL can survive as a total independent. Now Europe's seventh largest producer and slipping, BL is too far behind in a too competitive industry. More joint models such as the Honda and more bought-in components, even complete power trains, seem very much on the cards for BL. And whilst throughout the 1970s BL had problems producing enough quality Rovers, Jaguars, Triumphs and MGs to meet demand, demand in this sector is likely to become increasingly competitive. Not only are the Japanese moving up-market, but in the 1980s down-sized American cars are much closer substitutes than the earlier American luxury cars. As for Peugeot-Chrysler, prognostications are impossible so early in the venture. Peugeot successfully absorbed Citroën and integrated its model line with Peugeot. Perhaps it will do the same with Chrysler. On the other hand, other manufacturers, notably BL but also Chrysler itself, found the rationalisation of a number of different philosophies and model lines impossible. Peugeot's task is awesome.

As far as the whole British motor industry is concerned, certain developments are likely to continue. First, there will be more component production and less assembly in Britain. Secondly, as discussed in Chapter 7, a truly successful components industry depends upon there being a home industry for base supply. Perhaps BL and the multinationals will provide this base and continued expansion in this sector continue. If not, some further contraction of the UK motor industry, including components, is to be expected. But there is a minimum scale to which the industry is likely to shrink. The UK car market is still an important one by world standards. Importers are highly aware of their impact on the UK balance of payments. Austria, Australia, Canada, South Africa and a host of other countries have local content laws of some sort. Usually countries require that a certain proportion of a car be produced locally, but will allow vehicles with less local content to be imported without tariff penalties if the producer exports locally-made component parts of equal value. Should the UK components industry also collapse, the UK would likely be impelled to introduce local content laws. It is hoped that the UK components industry will expand on merit in any case. If not, it is likely to continue as a supplier of components simply to offset, in part at least, the UK balance of trade deficit in cars which will almost certainly characterise the 1980s.

The labour force in the motor industry worldwide is likely to decline in the 1980s as machines replace men. It is estimated that in the United States the labour force will fall by 128,000 by 1985.[8] In the over-manned UK motor industry, with a declining share of world markets, attrition is essential. This is already slowly underway. In 1978 BL trimmed its labour force by 12,000.[9] But circumstances of decline are not generally favourable for improved labour relations, so poor labour relations are likely to continue to plague the motor industry.

Disenchanted with economic intervention, less concerned with the balance of payments thanks to North Sea oil, to some extent constrained by EEC commitments, with less unemployment probable in the 1980s due to demographic factors, and with the motor industry in any case less important than it was once upon a time, government involvement in the UK motor industry is likely to be less in the 1980s than in previous years. Many of the options which characterised government intervention since 1945, particularly demand management policies using the motor industry, are no longer open.

Finally, it is interesting to speculate very briefly about where the UK motor industry might have been had government policy been more successful. If it is assumed that the UK motor industry had grown in line with other European nations since 1960, then its size in 1979 might have been about the same as the French. Whilst such speculation is, in the main, futile, such growth could have meant that the current industry workforce, assuming productivity levels approximately equal to European levels, could have produced all the increased output. Such a development would have had favourable effects on the balance of payments. French exports in 1978 totalled 7.6 billion pounds in value versus UK exports worth 3.4 billion pounds. The difference, unrealistically ignoring any impact on import levels, would have improved the UK balance of payments by about 3.2 billion pounds, a contribution of about the same magnitude as that generated by North Sea oil. Also, of course, job security and pay in the industry would have been better, for the present. But in the 1980s competition in the European motor industry will be intense, as noted above. Already we have noted, for reasons only partly related to government policies, Britain for many years has not had a comparative advantage in car production. Particularly the UK lacks a segment in the labour force that knows poverty in the way guest workers do in France, Germany and Italy, or Southern blacks do who move to Detroit in the United States. Such a memory seems to make motor factory conditions bearable. In other words, even if the UK motor industry had been more successful up until 1979, it would have still faced exceedingly difficult times in the 1980s. And, as we have noted before, there is some minimal size to which the UK motor industry is likely to shrink, based not so much upon economic considerations as political ones.

A Summing Up

In Chapter 1 I suggested that government policies that intentionally generated some relative decline in the UK motor industry might have been worthwhile if such policies contributed to the achievement of the country's overall goals. I have shown that in many specific instances the desired ends were not achieved to the extent intended whilst all too often the costs imposed exceeded those anticipated. In the aggregate, therefore, I conclude that the sacrifices were not worthwhile. Overall, government policy dealing with the UK motor industry between 1945 and 1979 was a failure.

At the outset I justified this review of the effects of government policy on the UK motor industry on the grounds that it could provide lessons for the future. I have attempted to show how, over the years, a number of policies, the majority of seemingly limited scope, had, in the aggregate, very considerable and far-reaching consequences for the

UK motor industry. Furthermore, the often pernicious consequences of government policy were felt long before the Ryder and Lever Reports of 1975, the BL toolmakers' strike of 1977 and the Peugeot takeover of Chrysler in 1978 made crisis in the motor industry a regular media event. Indeed these regular crises in the seventies can be seen largely as the results of developments, often government-inspired, over the previous quarter of a century.

Already in the UK in the late seventies the government, whether Labour or Conservative, appeared to be more cautious in introducing policies, be it demand management or specific industrial strategies, that might jeopardise productive efficiency in the motor industry or other industries. Similar trends of caution can be discerned in some other Western countries. The evidence presented here about the government's role in the UK motor industry's decline suggests that the move to more circumspect government involvement and planning in dealing with any specific industry is a desirable one.

Notes

1. D.T. Jones and S.J. Prais, 'Plant Size and Productivity in the Motor Industry: Some International Comparisons', *Oxford Bulletin of Economics and Statistics*, vol. 40 (May 1978), pp. 131-51.
2. *Financial Times*, 2 Feb. 1978.
3. *Business Week*, 30 Oct. 1978, p. 49.
4. *Fortune*, 7 May 1979, p. 125.
5. Ibid., 20 Nov. 1978, p. 102.
6. *The Economist*, 8 July 1978, p. 99.
7. *Sunday Telegraph*, 10 June 1979.
8. *The Economist*, 10 June 1978, p. 91.
9. *Sunday Telegraph*, 10 June 1979.

SELECTED BIBLIOGRAPHY

Books

Allen, C.C. *British Industries and Their Organization* (Longman, London, 1970)

— *The Structure of Industry in Britain* (Longman, London, 1970)

Bagwell, P.J. *The Transport Revolution* (Batsford, London, 1974)

Bain, J. *Barriers to New Competition* (Harvard University Press, Cambridge, Mass., 1956)

— *Industrial Organization* (Wiley, New York, 1968)

Beynon, H. *Working For Ford* (Allen Lane, Harmondsworth, 1973)

Buchanan, C. *Traffic in Towns* (Penguin, Harmondsworth, 1964)

— *Mixed Blessing: The Motor in Britain* (Penguin, Harmondsworth, 1967)

Cook, P.L. *Effects of Mergers* (Allen and Unwin, London, 1958)

Denton, G., Forsythe, M. and Maclennan, M. *Economic Planning and Policies in Britain, France and Germany* (Allen and Unwin, London, 1968)

Duncan, W.C. *US-Japan Auto Diplomacy: A Study in Economic Confrontation* (Ballinger, Cambridge, Mass., 1973)

Edwards, C.E. *Dynamics of the United States Automobile Industry* (University of South Carolina Press, Columbia, 1965)

Gwilliam, K.M. *Transport and Public Policy* (Allen and Unwin, London, 1964)

Hopfinger, K.B. *The Volkswagen Story* (Foulis and Company, Henley, 1971)

Maxcy, G. *The Motor Industry* (Allen and Unwin, London, 1959)

Maxcy, G. and Silbertson, A. *The Motor Industry* (Allen and Unwin, London, 1958)

Mishan, E.J. *The Costs of Economic Growth* (Praeger, New York, 1967)

Plowden, W. *The Motor Car and Politics, 1896-1970* (The Bodley Head, London, 1971)

Pratten, C.F. *Economies of Scale in Manufacturing Industry* (Cambridge University Press, Cambridge, 1971)

Rhys, D.G. *The Motor Industry: An Economic Survey* (Butterworths, London, 1972)

Richardson, K. *The British Motor Industry 1896-1939: A Social and Economic History* (Macmillan, London, 1977)

Scherer, F.M. *Industrial Market Structure and Economic Performance* (Rand McNally, Chicago, 1970)

Turner, G. *The Car Makers* (Eyre and Spottiswoode, London, 1963)

— *Business in Britain* (Eyre and Spottiswoode, London, 1969)

Turner, H.A., Clack, G. and Roberts, G. *Labour Relations in the Motor Industry* (Allen and Unwin, London, 1967)

White, L.J. *The Automobile Industry Since 1945* (Harvard University Press, Cambridge, Mass., 1971)

Government Publications

Central Policy Review Staff *The Future of the British Car Industry* (HMSO, London, 1975)

HM Treasury 'Report on the Motor Industry Joint Working Party' (unpublished paper, London, 1974)

— 'The Operation of Monetary Policy Since the Radcliffe Report' (*Bank of England Quarterly Bulletin*, February 1969)

Monopolies Commission *Report on Equipment for the Motor Industry* (HMSO, London, 1963)

— *Report on Wire Harnesses for the Motor Industry* (HMSO, London, 1966)

National Advisory Council to the Motor Manufacturing Industry *Report on Proceedings* (HMSO, London, 1947)

National Economic Development Office *Growth of the United Kingdom to 1966* (HMSO, London, 1963)

— *The Effect of Government Policy on the Motor Industry* (HMSO, London, 1968)

— Motor Manufacturing Economic Development Council for the Motor Industry *Regional Policy and the Motor Industry* (HMSO, London, 1969)

— *Economic Assessment to 1972* (HMSO, London, 1971)

— *Japan: Its Motor Industry and Market* (HMSO, London, 1971)

— *Motors: Industrial Review to 1977* (HMSO, London, 1973)

— *The Increased Cost of Energy — Implications to United Kingdom Industry* (HMSO, London, 1974)

— Motor Manufacturing Economic Development Council *Motor Industry Statistics* (HMSO, London, various years)

Parliament (Commons) *The National Plan* (Command 2764, 1965)

Parliament (Commons) *British Leyland: The Next Decade* (HMSO, London, 1975)

Parliament (Commons) *Fourteenth Report of the Expenditure Committee 1974-75: The Motor Vehicle Industry* (HMSO, London, 1975)

Parliament (Commons) *Eighth Report of the Expenditure Committee, 1975-76: Public Expenditure on Chrysler (UK)* (HMSO, London, 1976)

Parliament (Commons) *The Bullock Report: The Report of the Committee of Inquiry into Industrial Democracy* (HMSO, London, 1977)

Journals and Articles

Ali, M.A. 'Hire Purchase Controls and the Post-war Demand for Cars in the United Kingdom', *Journal of Economics Studies*, 1 (Jan. 1965)

Armstrong, A.C. 'The Motor Industry and the British Economy', *District Bank Review*, 164 (Sept. 1967)

Ball, R.J., Eaton, J.R. and Steven, M.D. 'The Relationship Between United Kingdom Export Manufactures and the Internal Pressure of Demand', *Economic Journal*, 76 (Sept. 1966)

Boyle, S.E. 'A Blueprint for Competition: Restructuring the Motor Vehicle Industry', *Journal of Economic Issues*, IX (June 1975)

Bressly, M. 'Changing Locational Advantages in the United Kingdom Motor Industry', *Journal of Industrial Economics*, V (Oct. 1957)

Cowling, K. and Cubbin, J. 'Price, Quality and Advertising Competition: An Econometric Analysis of the United Kingdom Car Market', *Economica*, 38 (Sept. 1971)

Cowling, K. and Rayner, A.J. 'Price, Quality and Market Share', *Journal of Political Economy*, 78 (Oct. 1970)

Cubbin, J. 'Quality Change and Pricing Behaviour in the United Kingdom Car Industry, 1956-68', *Economica*, 41 (Feb. 1974)

Galambros, P. 'The Effects of Controls on UK Sates, 1952-1960', *Yorkshire Bulletin*, XIV (May 1961)

Jones, D.T. and Prais, S.J. 'Plant Size and Productivity in the Motor Industry: Some International Comparisons', *Oxford Bulletin of Economics and Statistics*, vol. 40 (May 1978)

Salmon, E.A. 'Inside British Leyland', *Management Today*, 114 (Nov. 1975)

Silbertson, A. 'The Motor Industry, 1955-64', *Oxford Bulletin of Economics and Statistics*, XXVII (Nov. 1965)

— 'Hire Purchase and the Demand for Cars', *Economic Journal*, 72 (Mar. 1963)

Walker, G. 'Competition in Transport as an Instrument of Policy', *Economic Journal*, LXIV (Sept. 1956)

Williamson, O.E. 'Towards a National Exchange Policy: Some Reflections on British Experience', *Bulletin of the Reserve Bank of St. Louis* (Apr. 1969)

Wykoff, F.A. 'A User Approach to New Automobile Purchases', *Review of Economic Statistics*, 40 (June 1973)

Newspapers and Other Sources

Daily newspapers, weeklies and other magazines were a major source of information and included:

Autocar, Business Monitor, Business Week, Challenge, Daily Express, Daily Mail, Daily Telegraph, Financial Times, Fortune, Guardian, Harvard Business Review, Investors Chronicle, Labour Gazette, Lloyds Bank Review, Management Today, Motor, Motor Business, Motor Sport, Motoring Today, New Statesman, Observer, Scotsman, Spectator, Sunday Telegraph, Sunday Times, The Economist, The Listener, The Times, Time, Weekly Guardian, Which?

In addition, considerable use was made of Company Reports, Bank Reviews, other government publications, and statistics from the Society of Motor Manufacturers and Traders, particularly their detailed annual publication, *The Motor Industry of Great Britain*.

INDEX